PRAISE FOR *THE WAR FOR TALENT*

"Any executive who doesn't view people as the greatest corporate asset should read *The War for Talent* to understand that their only protection against the forces of destruction is the best people—period."
    —Bob Beauchamp, President and CEO, BMC Software, Inc.

"In a young company, ensuring that you have the best people propelling the business is arguably a leader's most important obligation. Filled with clear, timeless philosophies, this book combines practicality with heart to give leaders a real guide to leveraging a company's ultimate competitive advantage—the talent of its people."
    —Kenny Feld, President and CEO, Contrado, Inc.

"A truly great book. Without talent, organizations are empty shells. Any organization without a compelling strategy for talent is heading for the precipice."
    —Sir Richard Evans, Chairman, BAE Systems plc

"*The War for Talent* is a refreshing book, offering sound practical advice for every manager. This book presents five actions that leaders must take to strengthen their talent pools. It is also very suitable for managing business in Europe. It is not only well written but also warmhearted and hard-driving."
    —Jacob Wallenberg
        Chairman of SEB and Executive Vice Chairman of Investor AB

"Finally, a book that presents a burning case for having a talent mindset. Leaders have to think and act differently to win the war for talent. This is a must-read for those who are serious about winning!"
    —Ursula Fairbairn, Executive Vice President of
        Human Resources and Quality, American Express

"Normally, the consulting fee for the advice given in this book would be very high indeed. It distills—on a clear, what-to-do basis—the key strategic element for sustainable growth in the decades to come. A must-read for any manager."
    —A. Daniel Meiland
        Chairman and CEO, Egon Zehnder International

"At GE, we have always believed that putting great people in critical positions is fundamental to business success. Using a rich blend of persuasive data and provocative anecdotes, this book embellishes that simple premise with real operational strategies for attracting and leveraging talent in an organization. It is both an interesting and very useful read."

—William J. Conaty, Senior Vice President, Human Resources, General Electric Company

"We all know that, in the end, it is people who will determine the success of any enterprise. The war for talent is constant, and this book gives us the tools to fight this war. Can there be anything more useful?"

—Shelly Lazarus, CEO, Ogilvy & Mather Worldwide

"*The War for Talent* has become the most talked-about study—now book—in the human capital space. 'Must-read' is much too mild an endorsement."

—Pat Pittard, Chairman, President, and CEO, Heidrick & Struggles

"A brilliant battle plan. *The War for Talent* is a major wake-up call to anyone in management—in small companies as well as large—whose success increasingly depends on being surrounded by talented individuals."

—John Darden, former President, Young Presidents' Organization Worldwide

"McKinsey's first studies in the 'war for talent' immediately made that phrase a part of the language of business. This pathbreaking continuation details why developing and managing the best talent ought to be a central part of every company's business strategy."

—Peter Cappelli, George W. Taylor Professor of Management and Director of The Center for Human Resources, The Wharton School, University of Pennsylvania

"Board members should encourage not just CEOs but senior leaders throughout the organization to make improving their talent pool a top priority. This book gathers essential tools managers need to measure and improve their all-important focus on talent management."

—Adam Clammer, Kohlberg Kravis Roberts & Co.

"This book hits the big sweet spot in today's competitive environment. *The War for Talent* is a must-read for any CEO."

—Jim Robbins, President and CEO, Cox Communications

THE WAR
FOR TALENT

THE
WAR
FOR
TALENT

Ed Michaels

Helen Handfield-Jones

Beth Axelrod

Harvard Business School Press Boston, Massachusetts

Requests for permission to use or reproduce material from this book
should be directed to permissions@hbsp.harvard.edu, or mailed to
Permissions, Harvard Business School Publishing, 60 Harvard Way,
Boston, Massachusetts 02163.

Library of Congress Cataloging-in-Publication Data

Michaels, Ed
   The war for talent / Ed Michaels, Helen Handfield-Jones, Beth Axelrod.
      p. cm.
   Includes bibliographical references and index.
   ISBN 1-57851-459-2
      1. Executive ability. 2. Leadership. 3. Employee motivation.
4. Employee retention. 5. Personnel management. I. Handfield-Jones, Helen
II. Axelrod, Beth III. Title.
   HD38.2 .M53 2001
   658.4'07--dc21

                                                           2001024864

The paper used in this publication meets the requirements of the American
National Standard for Permanence of Paper for Publications and Documents
in Libraries and Archives Z39.48-1992.

We dedicate this book to Joanie, Tom, and Erwin. Without your encouragement we never would have had the courage or the confidence to take on this somewhat surreal and seemingly endless project. Without your love and support, we never would have finished it.

CONTENTS

PREFACE

In the last week of November 1997, we were crammed into a conference room in the New York McKinsey office, mulling over stacks of data. We had sent out questionnaires to senior managers in seventy-seven large companies and had received more than 6,000 completed questionnaires back. In addition, we had conducted in-depth case studies with eighteen highly regarded companies. We had set out to learn how the best companies build a strong managerial talent pool and whether better talent drives company performance. Now we were struggling to make sense of all that we had collected. We had expected higher performing companies to have better HR processes, but this wasn't the case. On question after question related to formal processes, higher performing companies and average companies scored the same.

As we sifted through the reams of data, we began to discuss an interview we'd had earlier that week with Kevin Sharer, at the time COO (now CEO) of Amgen. Kevin had been struggling with how to persuade his managers to think about managing talent the way he did. "I told my leaders that if they believed that people are the responsibility of HR, they've totally missed the point," he said.

With that statement in mind, we began to reflect on similar discussions we'd had at Enron, Intel, Johnson & Johnson, The Home Depot, and General Electric. In each case, the corporate leaders had not spoken to us about their succession planning process, their evaluation process, their hiring process, their compensation process—or any other HR processes.

What they had spoken so passionately about was their belief that talented people were critical to their company's performance and success. Furthermore, they had described the bold actions they had been taking to strengthen their company's talent pools.

We looked at one another and suddenly the light bulb blinked on: It wasn't better HR *processes* that made the difference. Rather, it was the *mindset* of leaders throughout the organization that made the difference. That was the element we had underestimated.

Now the data began to make sense. What distinguished the high-performing companies from the average-performing was not better HR processes, but the fundamental belief in the importance of talent. It was also the actions they took to strengthen their talent pools.

Since that realization, we have observed time and time again the fundamental importance of a talent mindset. Without this mindset, recruiting becomes an activity. Development happens by serendipity. Average managers are tolerated in key spots. Attrition increases. Performance suffers.

At the outset of the project, our colleague Steven Hankin excitedly suggested the title "The War for Talent" for the final report that we would write. We all thought it was a good title, though perhaps too militaristic. Before we could talk ourselves out of it, though, we had printed 20,000 questionnaires with "The War for Talent" emblazoned on them and sent them out to senior managers across the business community. In retrospect, we're glad we did: The title vividly captures the new realities of the talent market.

In 2000 we launched a second round of research, this time with thirty-five large companies and nineteen medium-sized companies. We also revisited five of our eighteen original case study companies and added nine new companies. The twenty-seven companies we have studied in depth are described in the next section, "About the War for Talent Research."

Of all the findings from this second round of research, the lack of focus among companies on talent issues struck us as the most surprising. Despite all the media coverage and management rhetoric about the war for talent, only one in four companies made strengthening its talent pool a top priority. We could prove analytically that better talent leads to better performance, but many companies were missing this opportunity.

Our analytical research and case studies have provided us with a rigorous understanding of what comprises great talent management. Our experience serving clients has shown us firsthand how challenging it is for companies to make progress on this front. We have listened to numerous CEOs ponder the leadership gaps that constrain their companies' performance. We have counseled scores of line managers as they aspire to raise the level of talent in their organizations. We have observed many others who fail to recognize this opportunity. We have strategized with senior HR executives as they have attempted to reposition their HR functions as strategic thought partners to line leaders. Almost all the managers we have talked with recognize the benefits of strengthening their organization's talent pool. However, many don't know how to do it. They don't know how to get the momentum of their organizations behind the effort.

We wrote this book to address that need. We wanted to show leaders that great talent management is not about formal HR processes, but about their own beliefs, convictions, and actions. We wanted to show them that because of the persisting war for top managerial talent, the way they have managed talent in the past will not be sufficient in the future. We wanted to show them that with courage and conviction they *can* strengthen their talent pools and thereby achieve substantial performance improvements.

Indeed, we know they can. Over the last three years, our firm has helped more than 100 companies around the globe improve their talent management. We have seen firsthand the performance improvements they have achieved as a result.

Who Should Read This Book

This book is about how to attract, develop, excite, and retain highly talented managers. It is written for leaders at all levels of the organization—people who are striving to build a stronger managerial talent pool in their units, whether they are a CEO, a division president, a department head, a project team leader, or a store manager. This book is intended for any leader, in any organization, who manages people and affects the success and careers of others. While this book is addressed primarily to line and functional leaders, HR leaders should also find it valuable in their new, more strategic roles.

Although our research has been focused on U.S. companies, we believe that the principles in this book can be applied elsewhere. Half of our client work has been with companies outside the United States, and we have found that, with some tailoring to local cultures and practices, the principles are equally applicable.

We also feel that the principles in this book are pertinent to not-for-profit and public-sector organizations, ranging from academic institutions to the military. They are also applicable to talent other than managerial talent. For instance, the imperatives companies should adopt for electrical engineers and computer science grads are very similar to the ones outlined in this book (as discovered by a recent McKinsey research project).

What Is Talent?

What do we mean by *talent*? In the most general sense, talent is the sum of a person's abilities—his or her intrinsic gifts, skills, knowledge, experience, intelligence, judgment, attitude, character, and drive. It also includes his or her ability to learn and grow.

Defining great managerial talent is a bit more difficult. A certain part of talent eludes description: You simply know it when you see it. There is no universal definition of an outstanding manager, for what is required varies to some extent from one company to another. Each company must understand the specific talent profile that is right for it. A highly successful manager at The Home Depot might not fit the talent profile Enron needs. We can say, however, that managerial talent is some combination of a sharp strategic mind, leadership ability, emotional maturity, communications skills, the ability to attract and inspire other talented people, entrepreneurial instincts, functional skills, and the ability to deliver results.

Despite some blurry lines around the concept, talent is a seductive word, one which people seem to implicitly understand. And they wonder about their relationship to it: Am I "talent"? How do I increase my talent?

The word *talent* itself dates to antiquity and has a rich history. To the ancient Hebrews, Greeks, and Romans, a talent was a unit of weight. Through exchange of precious metals of that weight, it became a unit of monetary value. What is today a key source of value creation was, thousands of years ago, money. It has come full circle.

The term took on broader meaning in the New Testament's Parable of the Talents, in which St. Matthew recounted the tale of the lord who entrusted eight talents to his three servants. He gave five talents to the first servant, two to the second, and one to the last. The first two servants worked hard and doubled the value of their talents. The third was lazy and buried his talent in the ground. When the lord returned, he rewarded the first two servants for their enterprise and banished the third. The moral is that talent is a gift that must be cultivated, not left to languish.

In the sixteenth century, Martin Luther interpreted this parable to mean it is God's will that people exercise their innate talents through hard work, thus forming the basis of the Protestant work ethic. The meaning of talent, then, has grown in abstraction—from a unit of weight to a unit of money to a person's innate abilities to gifted people collectively. In this book it is code for the most effective leaders and managers at all levels who can help a company fulfill its aspirations and drive its performance.

As in ancient times, talent has become the coin of the realm. Companies that multiply their human talents will prosper. Companies that don't will struggle.

So we write this book for the millions of managers around the world. We hope it inspires you to develop the individual talents of the people around you, and hope it guides you to strengthen the collective talent of your organization.

ACKNOWLEDGMENTS

Conventional wisdom says that a committee can't write a book. Perhaps that is true, but a team can. We have had the great privilege of writing this book as a team. Beyond the three authors, our team included five people who went through every step of the journey with us: Erik Calonius, Jennifer Futernick, Katie Michaels, Lynn Heilig, and Pauline Williams.

We couldn't have been more blessed to have Erik Calonius as our primary editor. From the outset, he emphasized that "clear writing is clear thinking" and, in a masterful way, helped us with both sides of that equation. To the extent that this book is well paced and appears seamlessly written by three authors, Erik deserves much of the credit. He was the perfect editor, but beyond that, he was a brilliant coach and a delight to work with.

Jennifer Futernick, our secondary editor, encouraged us to write a book that engages as well as instructs, is timeless as well as timely, and is about people as well as companies. Jennifer served as our conscience, pushing us to make points more truthfully and with deeper insight, and she added clarity and color to our writing. In addition to helping research and write a number of the case stories, Jennifer served as a counselor and warmhearted friend to all on the team.

Katie Michaels is a terrific writer who, along with her mentor Jennifer, researched and wrote more than half of our case stories. She brought to the stories a sense of theater and wit that we could not have done ourselves. Katie also diligently nailed down many key points to complete the stories. It was a pleasure to have Katie on our team, but for Ed it was a special privilege because Katie is his daughter.

Lynn Heilig was responsible for our survey facts and secondary research. She was incredibly resourceful in uncovering information from sources we could never have tapped on our own, and was vigilant in ensuring the accuracy of every fact and reference. A friend and colleague for many years, Lynn has helped in innumerable ways to build our War for Talent practice.

We certainly could not have made it through this year without the immense help of Pauline Williams. A consummate professional, Pauline typed draft after draft of many chapters (often from nearly unintelligible scribbles) and coordinated the production of each major draft of the book.

Of course, every book is the product of myriad contributors. We began our journey with Steven Hankin, Libby Chambers, Stephanie Durr, Matthias Lingnau, and several other McKinsey colleagues who worked with dedication on the 1997 War for Talent research. Additionally, Larry Kanarek helped us think about the broader forces driving the war for talent and spent untold hours helping us sharpen our thinking for the final report of the 1997 research.

Tim Welsh led the War for Talent 2000 research team in its critical first months, led the Value of Talent research, and plays a leadership role in the War for Talent practice. Daniel Dowd, Tasha McNutt, Roy Messing, Jennifer Myung, and Jonathan Sipling worked tirelessly to analyze and synthesize the War for Talent 2000 Survey data. General research thanks also go to Jill Kern, John Roth, and Michelle Cafferty.

Without the companies that participated in our research, this book simply wouldn't exist. Our gratitude is boundless to the more than 100 companies that participated in our surveys, the 27 case companies that let us study them, and the more than 300 individuals we interviewed about their companies and their careers. We are particularly thankful to those people at the case companies who were uncommonly generous in helping us refine their stories.

Over the past several years we have learned a great deal from the many line executives, HR executives, academics, and executive search professionals we have had the privilege of meeting. Many of these people you will meet in the book, but we particularly want to thank Chuck Okosky, who until recently was Vice President of Executive Development at General Electric. Chuck has shared a lot of his practical wisdom with us—wisdom that only comes from years of experience at the coalface.

Two other guardian angels helped improve the quality of this book. Melinda Adams Merino, our editor at Harvard Business School Press, gave us many rounds of feedback, including a six-page memo in response to the first draft of our manuscript. On half a page she told us our book had promise, and on five and a half pages she gave us very specific and enormously helpful suggestions. Saul Rosenberg gave us important midcourse corrections after reading early drafts of our manuscript and helped us find our way to Harvard Business School Press and to Erik Calonius.

Tom Barkin, Parke Boneysteele, Lowell Bryan, Jonathan Day, Emily Hickey, Julian Kaufmann, Brook Manville, Dan Meiland, Bruce Roberson, and Jerome Vascellaro read early drafts of the manuscript and provided us with helpful feedback and advice. We thank them for the time and thoughtfulness they gave that task.

Finally, we thank our firm, McKinsey & Company, for allowing us to work on this book and to create the War for Talent practice over the past six years. Many thanks to the partners at McKinsey who trusted us to follow our passion. We hope this end product lives up to their trust.

Ed Michaels
Helen Handfield-Jones
Beth Axelrod

As I transition to retirement after thirty-two years with McKinsey & Company, I wish to pay tribute to my coauthors, trusted colleagues, and dear friends, Helen Handfield-Jones and Beth Axelrod.

Helen Handfield-Jones, having spent seven years researching organizations and serving clients full time, is a world-class expert on the broadest range of talent management issues. As our quarterback, Helen guided the structure of the book and shaped the direction of the final manuscript. She is a lucid thinker, splendid writer, and excellent consultant. This book would not have happened without Helen's passion, skill, and enthusiastic vision that we, in fact, had a book within us.

Beth Axelrod is among the best consultants I have worked with in my career. Drawing on her twelve years of experience serving clients on organization and talent management issues, Beth brought to this book a deep wisdom for just how hard it is to manage talent effectively. Beth's penetrating insights, razor-sharp intelligence, and compassionate touch can be felt both in the chapters she wrote and throughout this book. Beth has taken my place as the leader of the War for Talent practice.

Ed Michaels

ABOUT THE WAR
FOR TALENT RESEARCH

The perspectives we share with you in this book are drawn from three major research initiatives conducted by McKinsey & Company and led by the three authors: the War for Talent 1997 Survey, the War for Talent 2000 Survey, and talent management case studies done from 1997 to 2001. The surveys provide a quantitative understanding of what does and doesn't make a difference in building a strong talent pool. The case studies provide a rich qualitative understanding of how companies make great talent management happen—what it looks like in action.

We have also drawn on the findings of three other major research projects conducted by our McKinsey colleagues: the Value of Talent, the War for Technical Talent, and the Performance Ethic research.

Talent Management Case Studies

We chose companies for our cases that were, at the time, high-performing and had a reputation for strong talent. Some of the companies we chose have managed talent exceptionally well for many years. Some started to take a bolder, more rigorous approach to talent recently. Some were impressive turnaround stories both in terms of talent and financial results. A few were such spectacular growth stories that we figured they had to be doing something right on the talent front.

These are the twenty-seven companies we have studied as part of the 1997 or 2000 research or expressly for the purpose of this book:

AlliedSignal	HotJobs	PerkinElmer
Amgen	Intel	Sears, Roebuck and Co.
Arrow Electronics	Johnson & Johnson	SunTrust Banks
DoubleClick	Level 3 Communications	Symantec
Enron	Medtronic	Synovus Financial Corp.
General Electric	Merck & Co.	The Home Depot
Georgia-Pacific	Monsanto Company	The Limited Inc.
Harley-Davidson	Nabisco	U.S. Marine Corps
Hewlett-Packard	NationsBank	Wells Fargo

(AlliedSignal and NationsBank have since merged with other companies.)

Typically, we spent one to three days at these companies interviewing the CEO, several senior executives, the HR executive, and a few high-potential managers further down in the organization. Many of the impressive things we heard during these interviews we share with you in the pages of this book.

It's important to understand that none of these companies performs all aspects of talent management well. They might excel at one or more of the talent management imperatives and struggle with others. We do not present these companies as perfect exemplars, but rather as sources we can all learn from.

Some of our case companies will undoubtedly fall on hard times in the years ahead, for success is not assured solely through managing talent well. We recognize this, yet believe that the lessons we can learn from these companies are nevertheless enlightening.

Unless cited otherwise or footnoted, the company stories that appear in this book are based on our own interviews.

The War for Talent Surveys

We conducted the War for Talent Surveys to understand how companies build a strong pool of managerial talent—how they attract, develop, and retain the people in the top 200 managerial positions and how they build a pipeline of younger talent that might one day move into more senior positions.

We designed the survey to identify what the top-performing companies do differently from the average-performing companies when it comes to talent management. We defined top-performing companies as those in the top quintile of companies in their industry based on total returns to shareholders, and average-performing companies as those in the middle quintile.

In 1997, we invited many large U.S.-based companies (with more than $2 billion in sales) that had performed in the top quintile or the middle quintile of their industry to participate. Seventy-seven of them agreed. In 2000, we invited a wider range of U.S.-based companies to take part: large companies with revenue of more than $1 billion and midsized companies with revenue between $100 million and $1 billion. This time, we did not limit the sample to top-quintile or middle-quintile performance. Thirty five large companies and nineteen midsized companies agreed to participate in the 2000 survey. The companies that participated are listed in the appendix at the back of this book.

We asked hundreds of managers at each company to complete our questionnaires. One type of questionnaire went to the corporate officers, roughly the top twenty executives in each company. We asked them about the strength of their company's talent pool, how they think the company should manage talent, and how the company actually does manage talent. Another type went to senior managers, people in the 150 to 250 most senior management positions. We asked them to rate how well the company manages talent and we also asked them about their own careers: why they joined the company and remained with it; what has contributed to their development; and whether they are considering leaving the company.

In 2000, we added an additional group to our survey, young middle managers. We defined this group as people younger than thirty-five, in positions that typically lead to senior executive positions. We added this group because we wanted to learn how the perspective of future leaders differs from those of more senior people. We asked them the same kinds of questions we asked the senior managers.

In 1997, we also asked the senior HR executive to complete a questionnaire that described the practices, policies, and processes their company used for managing its senior managers.

The total numbers of companies and individuals that participated in the War for Talent Surveys are as follows:

	1997	2000
Number of companies		
Large companies	77	35
Midsized companies	none	19
Number of respondents		
Corporate officers	360	400
Senior managers	5,600	4,100
Midlevel managers	none	2,400
HR executives	72	none
Total respondents (excluding HR)	5,960	6,900

Throughout the book we quote the 2000 survey data—they are more recent and they include a broader set of questions than the earlier survey. In all cases where we have 1997 data and have shown 2000 data, the findings from both sets of data are consistent. The 2000 data we show includes only responses from the large companies. Responses from the large and midsized companies are very similar. Whenever we show data for high-performing and average-performing companies in this book, the differences in their mean scores are statistically significant.

More information about the War for Talent Survey methodology can be found in the appendix at the end of this book.

Limitations of the Research

Our research has been conducted primarily with private-sector, U.S.-based, large and midsized companies. We have not studied the talent practices of companies based outside the United States, start-ups, public-sector, or not-for-profit institutions.

Additionally, our research focuses exclusively on executive and managerial talent. By design, we did not study frontline or technical workers. The latter are covered in McKinsey's War for Technical Talent research.

THE WAR
FOR TALENT

1

THE WAR
FOR TALENT

I n 1997, we at McKinsey & Company coined the term *the war for talent* and soon realized we had named a phenomenon that many people had been experiencing but had not fully articulated. The forces shaping this war had been brewing for some time, then came to a head quite suddenly. Overnight, it seemed, everyone was talking about the war for talent.

The economy was burning white hot in the late 1990s and companies were scrambling to hire and retain the people they needed. Companies were offering large signing bonuses, employees were asking for raises three months after they joined, and headhunters were cornering hot recruits before they had even settled behind their desks. Many companies had hundreds of vacancies they couldn't fill, and some of the venerable bastions of talent (such as investment banks and consulting firms) were losing talent to dot-com upstarts. It was easy to see the war for talent raging in the recruiting and retention frenzy of the late 1990s.

Then the dot-com bubble burst, the Nasdaq crumbled, and fears of recession spread. As the economy cooled off it was easy to think that the war for talent was over. But the war for talent is far from over. In fact, we assert that it will persist for at least another two decades.

A Strategic Inflection Point

In his thought-provoking book, *Only the Paranoid Survive*, Andy Grove wrote that it's easy to miss the potential of new technologies, the impact of new competition, and the shifting power of customers and suppliers—critical points in time that Grove called *strategic inflection points*. For example, the ports of New York and San Francisco lost business by missing the shift to containerization, whereas the ports of Seattle and Singapore prospered. Likewise, Steve Jobs nearly ran his second computer company, NeXT, into the ground by ignoring the emergence of mass-produced, Windows-fueled PCs.[1]

We believe the war for talent is a similar strategic inflection point. It rose quietly from the ashes of the Industrial Age in the 1980s, jumped into the headlines in the 1990s, and will continue to reshape the workplace in the decades ahead.

It is an inflection point that says that *talent* is now a critical driver of corporate performance and that a company's ability to attract, develop, and retain talent will be a major competitive advantage far into the future. "The only thing that differentiates Enron from our competitors is our people, our talent," said Enron Chairman Kenneth Lay recently. "The whole battle going forward will be for talent. In fact, it has been that way for the last decade. Some people just didn't notice it."[2]

It seems like an easy message to understand, but many companies haven't fully grasped it. Like the ports of New York and San Francisco did, they are continuing with the status quo.

Although the war for talent rages on many fronts, this book is about the war for managerial talent: people who can lead a company, division, or function; guide a new product team; supervise a shift in an industrial plant; or manage a store with 15 or 150 associates. Managerial talent is not the only type of talent that companies need to be successful, but it is a critical one and it is at the epicenter of the war for talent.

The War for Talent Will Persist

There are three fundamental forces fueling the war for talent: the irreversible shift from the Industrial Age to the Information Age, the intensifying demand for high-caliber managerial talent, and the growing propensity for people to switch from one company to another. Since these structural forces show no sign of abating, we believe the war for managerial talent will be a defining feature of the business landscape for many years to come.

Irreversible shift from Industrial Age to Information Age

The war for talent began in the 1980s with the birth of the Information Age. With it, the importance of hard assets—machines, factories, and capital—declined relative to the importance of intangible assets such as proprietary networks, brands, intellectual capital, and talent.

Companies' reliance on talent increased dramatically over the last century. In 1900, only 17 percent of all jobs required knowledge workers; now over 60 percent do.[3] More knowledge workers means it's more important to get great talent, since the differential value created by the most talented knowledge workers is enormous. The best software developers can write ten times more usable lines of code than average developers, for example, and their products yield five times more profit.[4] Cisco CEO John Chambers put it this way: "A world-class engineer with five peers can outproduce 200 regular engineers."[5]

The shift to the Information Age is far from over. As the economy becomes more knowledge-based, the differential value of highly talented people continues to mount.

Intensifying demand for high-caliber managerial talent

In addition to this broad demand for talent, the demand for high-caliber managerial talent is growing. The job of managers is becoming more challenging as globalization, deregulation, and rapid advances in technology change the game in most industries.

Companies today need managers who can respond to these challenges. They need risk takers, global entrepreneurs, and techno-savvy managers. They need leaders who can reconceive their business and inspire their people.

Our War for Talent research shows just how hungry companies are for strong managerial talent. Ninety-nine percent of the corporate officers participating in our survey in 2000 said their managerial talent pool needs to be much stronger three years from now. Only 20 percent agreed that they have enough talented leaders to pursue most of their companies' business opportunities.[6]

In addition to the increased demand from established companies for highly capable managers, start-ups have added a whole new layer of demand on this talent pool. Though a number of talented managers have always been attracted to small companies, the flood of venture capital in the mid- to late 1990s and the burst of high tech and Internet business opportunities suddenly made small companies a hot destination. Since the Nasdaq crash in 2000–2001, the migration of talent has slowed and people probably have a more realistic view of the risks of going with a start-up. We believe, however, that start-ups and small companies will continue to absorb a fair amount of talent, particularly as the venture capital firms make seasoned managerial talent a prerequisite to investing. Ray Lane, a partner with Kleiner Perkins, comments on this shift: "The venture business is going to change enormously—from simply raising funds to teaching companies how to build a great management team and make the right deals."[7]

Meanwhile, the supply of managerial talent is limited. Although the size of the total workforce in the United States will grow a total of 12 percent over the ten years from 1998 to 2008, the number of twenty-five- to forty-four-year-olds—the demographic segment that will supply companies with their future leaders—will actually *decline* 6 percent during the same period.[8]

To some extent, companies could compensate for this decline in younger managers by relying on a greater number of older managers, because during this period the number of fifty-five- to sixty-four-year-olds will increase by more than 45 percent.[9] This, however, will leave companies even more exposed when these older managers retire in large numbers during the second decade of the millennium. Although some older managers might be enticed to stay in the workforce longer, it is far from certain that they will do so in large numbers. For the last twenty years, the average age of retirement has remained between sixty-two and sixty-three.[10]

Companies are already feeling the shortage of great managerial talent. "Leadership is the biggest single constraint to growth at Johnson & Johnson, and it is the most critical business issue we face," commented CEO Ralph Larsen, recently.[11] Similarly, Jim Robbins, CEO of Cox Communications, said in early 2000, "Talent is the single gating factor for us in realizing our growth vision."[12]

Over the coming two decades, then, companies will be competing intensely for the limited supply of very capable managers. Short-term fluctuations in economic activity will make the talent market a little looser or tighter from time to time, but the long-term trends are clear. In fact, it would take a substantial and long-lasting slump in the economy for this pressure to ease.

The executive search firms tell us that the demand for top managerial talent is still strong, despite the recent slowing in the economy. Revenues of two of the large, prestigious search firms grew at double-digit rates in 2000 and strong single-digit rates in the first quarter of 2001.[13]

Growing propensity to switch companies

Just as companies have come to recognize their need for highly skilled managers, however, managers have come to recognize the advantage of switching companies. It was the corporate downsizing of the late 1980s that first broke the traditional covenant that traded job security for loyalty. That was followed in the mid-1990s by a surge in job opportunities, and, coincidentally, greater transparency about those opportunities through Internet job boards and career sites. Within a few short years, the old taboos against job-hopping had evaporated and it had become a badge of honor to have multiple companies on one's resumé.

Today, many managers have become passive job seekers; they have their antennae up all the time for other opportunities. Our research shows the extent of this trend: 20 percent of managers said there is a strong chance they will leave their current company in the next two years, and another 28 percent said there is a moderate chance of leaving.[14] We also found that the challenge for companies is likely to get worse in the coming years: Younger managers are 60 percent more likely to leave than older managers.[15]

As Peter Cappelli said in *The New Deal at Work*, "While employers have quite clearly broken the old deal and its long-term commitments, they do not control the new deal. . . . It is hard to see what could make employees give that control and responsibility back to the employer."[16]

The structural forces driving the war for talent, then, are inexorable and widespread. The economic and demographic forces are replicated in many developed countries. The war for talent is creating a new business reality.

The Old Reality	The New Reality
People need companies	Companies need people
Machines, capital, and geography are the competitive advantage	Talented people are the competitive advantage
Better talent makes some difference	Better talent makes a huge difference
Jobs are scarce	Talented people are scarce
Employees are loyal and jobs are secure	People are mobile and their commitment is short term
People accept the standard package they are offered	People demand much more

Implications of the War for Talent

The structural forces fueling the war for talent yield two profound implications. First, the power has shifted from the corporation to the individual. More than ever, talented individuals have the negotiating leverage to ratchet up their expectations for their careers. The price for talent is rising.

Although this is good news for individuals, it presents yet another challenge for companies in the war for talent. Companies will have to work harder if they are going to win the battle for highly talented managers.

The second implication is that excellent talent management has become a crucial source of competitive advantage. Companies that do a better job of attracting, developing, exciting, and retaining their talent will gain more than their fair share of this critical and scarce resource and will boost their performance dramatically.

Our War for Talent research shows this. The companies that scored in the top quintile of our talent management index earned, on average, twenty-two percentage points higher return to shareholders than their industry peers. The companies that scored in the bottom quintile earned no more than their peers.[17] Certainly, many factors other than talent management are driving return to shareholders, but these data provide compelling evidence that better talent management results in better performance.

Clearly, having more capable people isn't the only thing companies will have to do to win. They will also have to set high aspirations and enact the right strategies and performance initiatives. They will have to energize and align all their people so they deliver their best performance. But talented leaders are needed to make these other performance drivers happen.

As companies respond to the war for talent, they will develop more powerful and more sophisticated approaches to talent management. Over the next decade we believe talent management will advance as far as marketing did in the 1960s and quality did in the 1980s. Some companies will advance in building this capability; others will fall behind.

It's intriguing that even the best companies are striving to improve the way they manage talent. When we launched the War for Talent research in 1997, we asked twenty-one companies with excellent financial performance and a reputation for great talent management to be our case studies. Most of these firms are asked daily to host best-practice visits, and they routinely reject the vast majority of such requests. Surprisingly, only three of the twenty-one we asked turned us down. The high acceptance rate had little to do with our persuasiveness and everything to do with their recognition that even they needed to raise their talent game. Indeed, they bordered on paranoia about the war for talent around them.

We therefore agree with Andy Grove's chilling mantra, "Only the paranoid survive." However, we will take the concept one step farther. Whereas Grove wrote that companies should be paranoid about the next wave of technology over the horizon or the next shift in markets, we think the greatest challenge will be whether a company can strengthen its talent pool dramatically enough and fast enough to stay ahead of the competition. *That* is the critical strategic inflection point that companies and managers must recognize and address.

Most Companies Have a Long Way to Go

A few companies have been managing talent effectively for some time, the most renowned being General Electric (GE), long admired for the strength and depth of its managerial talent. Most companies, though, have not managed talent effectively. Companies proclaim that people are their most important asset, but many don't act that way. Most companies struggle with talent management.

Figure 1-1 shows managers' perceptions of how well their company manages talent. As you can see, the scores are very low. Even if we were to add "somewhat agree" answers to these questions, the scores would still not be very good. More than half of the managers believe their company does *not* develop people quickly, retain high performers, or remove underperformers. Imagine if these were five

Figure 1-1 Most Companies Are Poor at Talent Management

% of senior managers who strongly agree that their company:

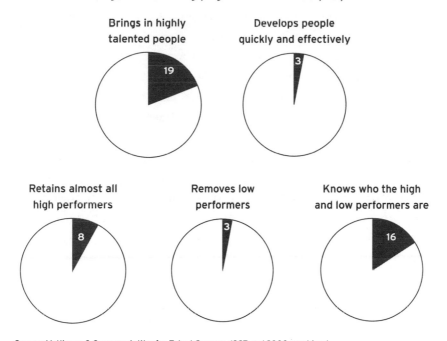

Source: McKinsey & Company's War for Talent Surveys, 1997 and 2000 combined

key questions about productivity, customer service, or quality—no company would accept such low scores.

It's not that companies aren't aware there is a war for talent: 72 percent of respondents strongly agreed it is critical their companies win the war for talent. However, companies haven't yet taken sufficient action: Only 9 percent are confident that the actions they are taking will lead to a stronger talent pool.[18]

Some companies are realizing that their current approaches to talent management are inadequate. "We spend four months per year on the budget process, but we hardly spend any time talking about our talent—our strengths and how to leverage them, our talent needs and how to build them," said Cox Communications CEO Jim Robbins. "Everyone is held accountable for his or her budget. But no one is held accountable for the strength of the talent pool.

Isn't it the talent we have in each unit that drives our results? Aren't we missing something?"[19]

Why have so few companies been successful in raising their talent game? Many have not consciously made the link between better talent management and business performance. Many have failed to make talent-building a priority: Only 26 percent of respondents said improving their talent pool is a top three priority in their company.[20] Virtually no company has held leaders at all levels accountable for the talent pool they build.

Is talent one of your top three priorities? How do you think your senior managers would rate your company on the five key questions in figure 1-1? There seems little doubt that most companies need to muster the courage and conviction to fundamentally change their approach to managing talent.

A Whole New Approach to Talent Management

In recent years numerous books have been written on the subject of talent management. Some discuss in depth the change in the relationship between companies and employees. Others suggest that companies structure their workforce into temporary and permanent groups of employees. Still others offer detailed advice on how to conduct recruiting interviews or design a leadership development program. Although all of these are useful topics, they are not what this book is about. Instead, this book offers a strategic view of the levers every company and every leader should pull to attract, develop, assess, excite, and retain highly talented managers.

We will show you what some very capable leaders have done to build the strength of their companies' talent pools. You will see how they came to understand that the war for talent is a strategic inflection point and how they realized that a stronger talent pool can be a crucial source of competitive advantage.

From our War for Talent Surveys of nearly 13,000 managers, our study of 27 case companies, and McKinsey's experience serving more than 100 companies and holding discussions with 100 more, we have identified five imperatives that companies need to act on if they are going to win the war for managerial talent and make talent a competitive advantage:

1. Embrace a talent mindset
2. Craft a winning employee value proposition
3. Rebuild your recruiting strategy
4. Weave development into your organization
5. Differentiate and affirm your people

1. Embrace a talent mindset

We found at GE, Enron, and Amgen—as well other companies we studied—a pervasive belief that performance and competitiveness are achieved with better talent. Without better talent, they know they won't outperform their competitors. Leaders up and down the line in these companies believe building their talent pool is a huge part of their job.

We've come to call this a *talent mindset*—the passionate belief that to achieve your aspirations for the business, you must have great talent. To have better talent, you must have every leader in the company committed to that goal. HR can't do the job alone. In short, more effective talent management is not about better HR processes; it's about a different mindset.

Most of the companies we surveyed do not have this mindset. At most companies, talent is *not* a top priority. Rather, people are HR's responsibility and managers make do with the talent pool they inherit. They consider talent to be only one of many levers, at best. These companies need to fundamentally change their definition of every leader's job. Larry Bossidy, former CEO of AlliedSignal, called finding and developing great leaders "the job no CEO should delegate."[21] We venture further and say that strengthening the talent pool is the job no leader at *any* level should delegate. The leverage of better talent is enormous.

Accountability for talent-building is essential to operationalize the talent mindset. In our War for Talent Survey we asked corporate officers, "*Should* line managers be accountable for the quality of their people?" Ninety-three percent responded that it is very important or critical for a company to do this in order to build a strong talent pool. However, when asked, "*Are* line managers held accountable for strengthening their talent pools?" only 3 percent strongly agreed.[22] Companies must address this inconsistency.

In chapter 2, "Embrace a Talent Mindset," you will see how a talent mindset has changed the way the CEOs of The Limited, PerkinElmer, and Amgen run their companies. We outline the six actions leaders must take to promote better talent management throughout their organizations. We also outline the dramatically new role HR leaders must play. We assert that the new breed of HR executives will be as important as the CFO. You will see what leaders at all levels with a talent mindset do and the difference this makes to their companies' performance.

2. Craft a winning employee value proposition

Every company has a customer value proposition; it is a clear, compelling reason why customers should do business with them. Few companies are nearly as thoughtful about why talented managers should join and stay with them. However, the new battlefield is as much for talented people as it is for key customers. Companies need to apply the same rigor to people management as they do to customer management.

What makes for a winning employee value proposition (EVP)? Talented managers want exciting challenges and great development opportunities. They want to be in a great company with great leaders. They want an open, trusting, and performance-oriented culture. And, yes, they want substantial wealth-creation opportunities. You can't make a great value proposition with money alone, but you can break one if the money isn't in the ballpark.

In chapter 3, "Craft a Winning Employee Value Proposition," you will learn more about what talented people are looking for. You will discover how DoubleClick, Enron, Synovus Financial, Level 3 Communications, and others have built powerful EVPs. Some of them are not in "sexy" industries, so they have had to make their companies exceptionally attractive. You will see how companies have tailored their EVPs to the type of people they are trying to attract and how they have leveraged the inherent strengths of their companies.

3. Rebuild your recruiting strategy

The recruiting game has changed dramatically. It's no longer about selecting the best person from a long line of candidates; it's about going out and finding great candidates. However, most companies use the same recruiting strategies they always have. They shop for candidates at the same five or six colleges. They search for the same kinds of people and hire in at the same levels. They may have started using the Internet as a recruiting tool, but they haven't changed much else.

We believe that companies must fundamentally rethink and rebuild their recruiting strategies. They should hire in at all levels— middle and senior as well as entry levels—which is a powerful way to inject new skills and new perspectives. They should also turn to new sources of talent. They should identify the intrinsic skills they need and then look for new faces from new places—from outside their industry and even from outside the business domain.

Aggressive companies are using new methods to find candidates, too. They are hunting for talent all the time, not just when they have vacant positions. They also understand that to woo people in today's talent market they have to sell, sell, sell. They make sure their high-performing line managers are the key recruiters. These companies also take advantage of cooler economic periods to capture top-notch talent that, at other times, is harder to win.

In chapter 4, "Rebuild Your Recruiting Strategy," you will see how The Home Depot, SunTrust Banks, and Arrow Electronics dramatically retooled their recruiting strategies and achieved striking results quite quickly.

4. Weave development into your organization

Winning the war for talent requires more than just winning the recruiting battle. Companies also have to make development a pervasive part of their company. Since there won't be enough fully developed managers to go around, every company and every leader will have to develop people to increase their capabilities. Development is also critical to attracting and retaining people. Talented people are inclined to leave if they feel they are not growing and stretching.

Many managers think development means training, but training is only a small part of the solution. Development primarily happens through a sequence of stretch jobs, coaching, and mentoring. At most companies these important development levers are insufficiently pulled. Divisional hoarding hampers development that comes through internal job moves: "I couldn't possibly let her go" is a common sentiment. Meanwhile, development through coaching and mentoring is left to serendipity. A few managers are good mentors and coaches, but most are not.

Companies need to fundamentally change the way they develop people by accelerating development and making it happen every day. They should match people to jobs in a much more deliberate way to optimize both development and performance. They should improve the frequency and candor of feedback and institutionalize mentoring. Every leader at all levels can and should be a people developer.

In chapter 5, "Weave Development into Your Organization," we will show you how GE, Amgen, Arrow Electronics, and the U.S. Marine Corps develop their people and how their techniques can be applied in your company as well.

5. Differentiate and affirm your people

We estimate that a large majority of managers have not had a written, candid performance review in years. We know that only 16 percent of the managers we surveyed said their companies really know who the high and low performers are.[23] How can companies promote and keep their most talented people if they don't systematically identify who they are? How can below-average performers be helped or moved if they aren't identified?

The better companies differentiate the pay, opportunities, and other investments that they make in people. They reward their best performers with fast-track growth and pay them substantially more than their average performers. They develop and affirm the solidly contributing middle performers, helping them raise their game. They remove weak players—believing that "blinking" on these hard decisions is unfair to the people working under that manager, to the organization at large, and even to the underperformers themselves. These companies have a very different ethic about what it means to manage their people.

Most companies struggle with differentiation. They don't have a way to identify the A, B, and C players and they don't have a disciplined process to make sure actions are being taken. Most companies conduct a one-day succession-planning event at the corporate level, but these exercises usually have little candor and little resulting action. The best companies have rigorous talent reviews in each division, which have the same intensity and importance as the budget process. The best companies decide on action plans for 100 to 500 individuals and plan to strengthen each division's talent pool. Then they follow up to make sure the actions happen.

In chapter 6, "Differentiate and Affirm Your People," we will show you how The Limited, National Australia Bank, and other companies do this and how you can institute a talent review process that will become the backbone of the way your organization manages talent. Taking deliberate action on A, B, and C players is how you can continuously upgrade your talent pool and, perhaps counterintuitively, make your company more attractive to talented people.

These five imperatives, taken together, represent a fundamentally new way of managing talent.

The Old Way	The New Way
HR is responsible for people management	All managers, starting with the CEO, are accountable for strengthening their talent pool
We provide good pay and benefits	We shape our company, our jobs, even our strategy to appeal to talented people
Recruiting is like purchasing	Recruiting is like marketing
We think development happens in training programs	We fuel development primarily through stretch jobs, coaching, and mentoring
We treat everyone the same, and like to think that everyone is equally capable	We affirm all our people, but invest differentially in our A, B, and C players

The Opportunity Awaits You

The war for talent is a strategic inflection point being missed by many companies. It will be a defining feature of the business landscape for many years to come. A temporary slowing of the economy will not reverse the inexorable trends driving the demand for highly talented people. The war for talent is a challenge for all companies, but for those that respond aggressively and early, it is also an enormous opportunity to gain competitive advantage.

In chapter 7, "Get Started—and Expect Huge Impact in a Year," we will help you understand your starting point and chart a course for the future. You will see from our many case studies that the talent journey is never ending, but that you can and should expect a huge impact in the first year of your effort.

You *can* win the war for talent. Imagine doubling your recruiting effectiveness. Imagine developing more of your people to their fullest potential. Imagine cutting your unwanted attrition rate in half. Imagine having more top performers and fewer below-average performers in your talent pool. Imagine the performance punch you would get by doing these things. Imagine the competitive advantage you would achieve if you truly had better talent throughout the ranks of your organization.

Responding aggressively to the war for talent will boost the performance of your organization—and make you a better leader as well.

2

EMBRACE A
TALENT MINDSET

L es Wexner is an extraordinarily talented and multifaceted man. He is a merchant, a lover of history, a philanthropist, and a devoted family man. Above all, however, he is an entrepreneur.

In 1963, after helping his parents run their store in a suburban Columbus, Ohio, shopping center, he started The Limited—so named because the store focused on clothing for younger women, unlike his parents' general merchandise store. Over the next twenty-five years he built a retailing and marketing marvel, which included The Limited, Express, Victoria's Secret, and Bath & Body Works. By 1990 he had 3,800 stores and $5 billion in sales; his company was named by *Fortune* as one of the "New Champs of Retailing."[1]

In the early 1990s, however, The Limited's earnings hit a wall and its stock plunged. Wexner was working harder than ever, but something was desperately wrong. He "went to war with himself" and decided to take counsel from several people he respected. He visited Steven Spielberg on the set of *Jurassic Park* to see how the famous director got his creative people to work together so well. He also visited GE's Jack Welch and Wayne Callaway, then the CEO of PepsiCo, to determine how they ran their businesses so well.

"I asked them how often they checked sales," Wexner recalls. "They said, 'Once or twice a month.' I checked ours twice a day. I asked them how much time they spent reviewing new ads. They said, 'Almost no time.' I asked them how much time they spent on new product concepts. They said, 'Occasionally—but only on a really big new product concept with a large capital expenditure.' I was spending half my time on products and ads."

Wexner was amazed. Finally he said, "Well, what *do* you do?" Separately, each of the men explained that they spent about half their time on people: recruiting new talent, picking the right people for particular positions, grooming young stars, developing global managers, dealing with underperformers, and reviewing the entire talent pool. Welch said to Wexner, "Having the most talented people in *each* of our businesses is the most important thing. If we don't, we lose."

By the time he had finished meeting with Spielberg, Welch, and Callaway, Wexner figured it out. He realized that the common element in all three success stories was *talent management*—how well these successful leaders had recruited, developed, and retained talented people. It was talent that made these companies great, Wexner saw, and it was talent that made them perform beyond their peers.

"It really was an epiphany," he says. "I discovered a completely different way of running a business."

When he returned home, Wexner immediately set his new talent mindset to work. First, he asked his HR managers for a list of The Limited's 100 most senior people. They didn't have one. Even after a list was created, Wexner realized he didn't know half the people on it well enough to assess them. "When I finished assessing them, I felt sick," he recalls. "I realized that my people weren't nearly as strong as they needed to be. I had hired other merchants like myself. We needed general managers, and we didn't have any."

Second, Wexner hired Len Schlesinger, a Harvard Business School organization professor, as a consultant and confidant (later he became COO and Executive Vice President of The Limited's Organization, Leadership, and Human Resources functions). They put together a talent review process that reviewed each division's talent strategies and the performance of the top 50 people in each division. Wexner not only attended all the meetings, he co-chaired them.

Third, Wexner began to pump new talent into the organization. He hired world-class general managers from Estée Lauder, Banana Republic, J. Crew, and The Gap. He also hired functional managers in finance, logistics, store operations, and information technology from Pillsbury, PepsiCo, and BellSouth. The newcomers brought deep experience and fresh perspectives—and with them came a new recognition of what outstanding talent looks like. They built their teams. Talented insiders got promoted and weak insiders were moved aside. Over those crucial three years, more than half of the people in the top 250 positions were changed. One-third of the replacements came from the outside and two-thirds came from the inside.

Within three years, the company's performance had improved dramatically. Profits had grown from $285 million to $445 million, and the company's stock price had almost doubled. To be sure, talent was not the only lever Wexner pulled. The portfolio was reshaped. Several divisions were closed, several were purchased, and several were spun off. Most notably, Victoria's Secret and Bath & Body Works were combined to create Intimate Brands, Inc. The merchandising process was fundamentally redesigned and the growth planning process was successfully installed. But, Wexner says, "Talent was the most important thing. Without better talent, most of the other actions would not have happened successfully."

Looking back on how his approach to managing the company had changed, Wexner declared, "I used to pick sweaters; now I pick people."[2]

It All Starts with a Talent Mindset

What Les Wexner learned was the most important lesson that we have learned in five years of discussions with hundreds of companies. Building a better talent pool is not about building a better HR department. It's not about better training. It's not about extending the annual succession planning meeting from one to two days. It's not about offering more stock options. It is about leaders and managers at all levels embracing a *talent mindset.*

Of the many prescriptions in this book, embracing a talent mindset is the most important. It is the starting point. Once a manager believes that talent is his or her responsibility, the other imperatives seem the logical and natural thing to do.

A talent mindset is the deep-seated belief that having better talent at all levels is how you outperform your competitors. It's the belief that better talent is a critical source of competitive advantage. It's the recognition that it is better talent that pulls all the other performance levers. Indeed, a talent mindset is the catalyst that activates the other talent-building imperatives.

Leaders with a talent mindset make talent management a huge and crucial part of their job. They understand it can't be delegated, so they commit a major part of their time and energy to strengthening their talent pool and helping others in the company strengthen theirs. Finally, leaders with a talent mindset have the passion, courage, and determination to take the bold actions necessary to strengthen their talent pools.

A talent mindset is strikingly different from the old thinking about people management.

Old Mindset About People	New Talent Mindset
A vague notion that "people are our most important asset"	A deep conviction that better talent leads to better corporate performance
HR is responsible for people management	All managers are accountable for strengthening their talent pool
We have a two-day succession planning exercise once a year	Talent management is a central part of how we run the company
I work with the people I inherit	I take bold actions to build the talent pool I need

In the rest of this chapter, we will show you how two other leaders adopted the talent mindset and strengthened their talent pools and how they helped others do the same. Furthermore, we will describe the six actions that leaders must take to make talent management a central part of their job.

A Talent Mindset Leads to Bold Actions

In our five years of conversations with hundreds of companies, we have never seen a company that has developed a pervasive talent mindset without the CEO's leadership and passion. While CEOs must have leaders beneath them who also believe passionately in the talent mindset, it must be driven from the top down. Spontaneous combustion from the bottom up does not seem to work. The CEO must set the tone, fix the standard, embody the passion, and demonstrate the courage to take bold actions. It takes a CEO, we have found, to light the bonfires throughout the company.

Greg Summe, CEO of PerkinElmer, is that kind of leader—one who has not only found the talent mindset himself, but who has spread it to others in his company.

That Summe is a successful business leader is not a surprise. The fifth of twelve children, he always had to scrape for his fair share, including sharing a bedroom with two or three siblings. Summe did well in high school and even better in his engineering classes at the University of Kentucky. Following college, he received a master's degree in electrical engineering from the University of Cincinnati and, eventually, an M.B.A. from the Wharton School of Business. After graduating in the top 5 percent of his class at Wharton, Summe decided to join McKinsey & Company, where he was elected partner.

After only two years as a partner, however, Summe surprised everyone when he announced that he was leaving McKinsey. First, he joined General Electric, and then AlliedSignal. Finally, in 1998 he got a call to become CEO of EG&G, a Boston-based engineering firm in thirty-one diverse businesses with sales of nearly $1.4 billion. For years, the company had been dependent on government contracts, but now sales were flat and profits barely acceptable. The situation demanded a new leader and a new direction.

Summe recognized that the company needed to do several things right away: become a dominant player in commercial sales, globalize its organization, form new alliances, and gain access to new technologies to compete in the global economy. To begin with, Summe got EG&G completely out of government contracting. Then he reorganized the company into four strategic business units: Life Sciences, Optoelectronics, Fluid Sciences, and Instruments. Summe also sold off eleven low-growth businesses and made nine acquisitions in high-growth sectors, adding $800 million in commercial sales. Simultaneously, he began to inject more of a performance focus into the company, including stretch targets for individuals and business units, real accountability for results, and new incentive plans. He also put better financial controls in place and launched initiatives to boost quality, productivity, and purchasing effectiveness. It was a textbook turnaround up to that point, but then he took it one step farther.

Having worked at McKinsey, GE, and AlliedSignal, Summe had come to realize the power of talent management. Acting on his talent mindset, Summe began to review the performance and potential of *every one* of the company's top people. "I not only assessed my fifteen direct reports, I started immediately to assess *their* direct reports," Summe recalls. "I met with each of them, probably 80 in all. I met with their people and asked about their leader, his or her leadership, their strategy, results, key issues, and the climate the leader created." Summe said the discussions were unbelievably revealing. "In about 30 minutes I could tell how effective the boss was, without even looking at the numbers."

Summe also hired Rich Walsh, an accomplished HR officer from Asea Brown Boveri, a European engineering conglomerate. With Walsh on board, the company developed a talent review process patterned after those of AlliedSignal and Asea Brown Boveri. "We drove the review process into every unit," says Summe. "I pushed my sector heads to strengthen their teams, and they in turn pushed and helped their people." Shawna Ward, Director of Marketing Communications and e-Business in the Life Sciences sector of the company recalls, "Greg challenged people who hadn't been challenged in years. He raised our aspirations, created excitement and energy, and brought in more capable people."

Indeed he did. At the end of his first year, Summe had reduced fifteen corporate officers to ten and replaced nine of those ten. Three sector heads, the CFO, the head of HR, and the head of corporate development were new to the company, each hired personally by Summe. Eighty percent of the top 100 employees were in new positions and half of them were new to the company.

Summe acknowledges that it is difficult to let people go, but he insists that it has to be done. "The most common mistake of leaders is that they stick with underperformers too long. People are naturally empathetic; they want everybody to succeed," he says. "But at some point you have to cut bait and move on. I think it's part of leadership to come to terms with your role in identifying the right skills for each key position. And you've got to make decisions and bring those skills in. Most of the people we moved out were intrinsically good human beings, but I knew they were not the right people to take us to the next level."

In addition to promoting forty insiders, Summe brought forty new hires into the top 100 positions. What kind of people did he promote and bring in? They were not only talented general managers and functional managers, but also people who could challenge and inspire others. They were people who themselves believed passionately in the talent mindset. They were managers like John Engel, who was hired away from AlliedSignal to be President of the Optoelectronics sector. In his first year as president, Engel moved sixty people into jobs that better suited their skills and hired forty high-level managers from the outside, many from competitors. "My job was to bring in talent and help develop talent that was much better than I was," Engel explains.

On October 26, 1999, Summe proudly rang the bell at the New

York Stock Exchange. It sounded the closing of the market and also announced to the world that the company had changed its name from EG&G to PerkinElmer (the name of one of the acquisitions). The hammer that Summe rang the bell with sits prominently on the bookshelf in his office today, a symbol of the fundamental changes that were made to the company.

The good news is that PerkinElmer's stock price has tripled in the three years since Summe joined EG&G. Was this due to classic restructuring alone? Summe thinks not. "If it hadn't been for our focus on talent management, it would not have worked," says Summe. "I would have gotten less than half of the results we saw in the first year—and even less going forward." He adds, "People were my number one issue three years ago. They are my number one issue now. And people will be my number one issue three years from now."

Like Greg Summe, leaders need to make talent management a very high priority. This is a distinguishing feature between high- and average-performing companies (see figure 2-1).

Figure 2-1 Make Talent a Top Priority

% of corporate officers who strongly agree

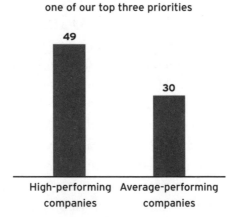

Improving the talent pool is
one of our top three priorities

49

30

High-performing   Average-performing
   companies   companies

Source: McKinsey and Company's War for Talent 2000 Survey

Talent Is Every Leader's Job

Whether you are a CEO, a division president, a plant manager, the head of the information systems department, a store manager, or the headmaster of a school, you have the opportunity to strengthen your pool of talent. Every leader should be asking, "How strong is my team, and what can I do to strengthen it?"

In addition to strengthening his or her own team, a leader has to make certain that talent is being strengthened throughout the organization. We have identified six actions a leader must take to exert his or her influence deeper into the organization:

- Establish the gold standard for talent.
- Get actively involved in people decisions deep within the organization.
- Drive a simple, probing talent review process.
- Instill a talent mindset in all managers throughout the organization.
- Invest real money in talent.
- Hold themselves and their managers accountable for the strength of the talent pools they build.

First, leaders establish a talent standard

As a leader, you must set the gold standard for talent for your organization. You do this implicitly every day through the quality of the people you hire, the quality of people you choose to keep in the company, and the standards you judge people against in their performance reviews. How often have you explicitly debated your organization's talent standard?

When we asked participants in our survey whether their senior managers share a common notion of what constitutes superior performance, only 10 percent agreed strongly that they did.[3] If senior leaders aren't clear on the characteristics of superior performance, how can they expect managers below them to be clear on the standards for talent and performance?

Larry Bossidy is one chief executive who does not leave the definition of superior talent to chance. When he came aboard as CEO of AlliedSignal in 1991, Bossidy knew he had to improve the quality of his manufacturing leaders. To begin the upgrading process, he described the kind of manufacturing leader he was looking for: one who would empower, not micromanage; lead, not administer; and understand technology, but not act like a technician.

Over the next two years, AlliedSignal used this profile to evaluate its top 400 manufacturing people. Those who measured up were given additional responsibilities. Those who didn't were encouraged to raise their game (though some couldn't meet the new standards). In two years AlliedSignal replaced 200 of its 400 manufacturing managers. This talent upgrade was part of a massive turnaround that helped raise AlliedSignal's stock price from $30 to $75 in less than three years.[4]

A gold standard for talent can be as simple as the sentence Larry Bossidy used to define manufacturing leaders, or it can be a comprehensive list of six to eight competencies (e.g., strategic thinking, communications skills, etc.), with a detailed description of the behaviors that characterize excellent, average, and poor performance for each one. Either way, the talent standard should sharply define the difference between poor, average, and excellent performance. It becomes the benchmark for evaluation and promotion across the organization, and a critical component of the talent mindset. Figure 2-2 shows that CEOs at high-performing companies play a larger role in setting the talent standard than at average-performing companies.

Second, leaders are actively involved in people decisions deep in their organization

Companies and leaders with a talent mindset believe that managerial talent belongs to the company *as a whole;* they view their top 100 to 500 managers as corporate assets. Furthermore, they realize

Figure 2-2   Establish a Gold Standard for Talent
% of corporate officers who strongly agree

CEO sets the standard
for the quality of people

Source: McKinsey and Company's War for Talent 2000 Survey

that talented people want to be considered for top jobs *across* the company.

This does not mean that these leaders *make* all the decisions on people two or three levels below them. They do get involved, however, by ensuring that the talent standard is being applied and by adding candidates to the slate being considered. When a vacancy is being filled, they interview the finalists, voice their opinions, then usually let the immediate boss make the decision.

The CEO, in particular, needs to be deeply involved in the deployment, development, recruiting, and retention of the top 100 to 500 people in the company. At PepsiCo several years ago, former CEO Wayne Callaway vetoed 30 percent of the "final" recommendations for openings in the top 500 and pushed the organization to look internally and externally for better candidates. One time, Callaway interviewed—not once, but twice—the two finalists for the Vice President of New Products position at Frito-Lay, a position three levels below him.[5]

A leader who constantly makes all the final hiring and promotion decisions two levels beneath will leave the other leaders feeling disenfranchised, but the other mistake—too little involvement—is more common. In fact, only 31 percent of the respondents in our War for Talent Surveys strongly agreed that their CEO "is actively involved in the assessment and movement of the top 200 managers."[6]

Fortunately, leaders such as Les Wexner and Greg Summe know how to handle this delicate balance. They share the decisions and, by getting involved, model and deepen the talent mindset.

Third, the leader drives a simple, but probing, review of talent

Do you regularly discuss the talent in your company with the same rigor and intensity that you discuss the budget? You should, yet only 18 percent of the corporate officers we surveyed strongly agreed that "our annual talent review process has the same intensity and importance as the budget process."[7] Leaders with such a talent mindset regularly conduct these kinds of discussions. The discussions result in firm action plans that describe how each unit will strengthen its talent pool.

Jack Welch, for instance, is renowned for spending thirty days each year chairing GE's talent review process (the famous "Session C"), in which the twenty to fifty general managers in each unit are discussed and action plans are developed. This process looks deeply at how talent is arrayed against critical business priorities, as well as the strength of the talent pipeline in each business. When people wondered how GE would fare without Jack Welch, Welch himself referred to the Session C process as an integral part of the GE operating system. He explained that the talent review process would outlive his tenure there and ensure that each leader and each organizational unit has a plan to strengthen its talent pool. Bill Conaty, Senior Vice President of HR, adds, "There is no question that Session C is GE's most defining process. Jack infused the process with his extraordinary vitality, but Session C actually predated Jack's election to CEO and will continue to be a critically important focus after his retirement."

You will read about the talent review process in detail in chapter 6.

Fourth, leaders instill a talent mindset in all managers throughout the organization

CEOs can't make it happen by themselves; they must instill the talent mindset in other leaders so great talent management happens at all levels. All the leaders in the organization must have a talent mindset. In fact, organizations that are outstanding at talent management have the mindset embedded in the institution. CEOs can make this happen by talking frequently with the other leaders about talent issues and by including talent management as one of the leadership competencies the company values.

Leaders should also demonstrate the mindset through their own behavior. However, only 9 percent of respondents in our surveys strongly agreed that "senior executives in our company model great talent management,"[8] and only 18 percent strongly agreed that senior executives view talent management as an important part of their job.[9] Contrast that with Jack Welch's view: "I view my primary job as strengthening our talent pools. So I view every conversation, every meeting as an opportunity to talk about our talented people, to learn about them, and to help them with their talent priorities. It's how we run GE." As one manager commented, "Every elevator ride with Jack is a Session C." This kind of continuous attention from the CEO sends a very powerful message about the importance of talent and whose role it is to manage it.

Do you give candid feedback to your direct reports on their performance and the ways in which they can improve? Do you address the issue of underperformers? Do you actively help your people shape their roles so they are constantly growing and stretching? Do you have a number of people outside your reporting line whom you actively mentor? If you are not doing these things, why would anyone else in your organization do them?

Fifth, leaders invest real money in talent

Because salaries, bonuses, and benefits hit the profit-and-loss statement immediately, many leaders are reluctant to invest aggressively

WHY HR LEADERS WILL BE AS IMPORTANT AS CFOS

Attracting, developing, and retaining talented people is the stuff of competitive advantage—more so than financing strategies, tax tactics, budgeting, or even some acquisitions. Hence, the HR leader has a much more strategic role to play in the years ahead, arguably one equal to that of the CFO.

In our research with corporate officers we asked, "Should HR be a high-impact partner to line managers in strengthening the talent pool?" Eighty-eight percent of respondents believed it is critical or very important that HR play that role. We then asked if their HR leader plays this role today, and only 12 percent strongly agreed.[10] Line managers want help from HR but most of them aren't getting it.

Every leader should indeed have much higher expectations for their HR managers. Each division and each major location should have a superb HR generalist who is strategic, impact-oriented, direct, tough-minded, and effective at influencing peers and senior managers. The following are some of the roles HR leaders should assume:

- *Help forge the link between business strategy and talent.* As John Engel of PerkinElmer says, "I expect my HR leaders to be fully engaged in driving growth and in being the strategic architects of our organization to support these growth strategies." When Julian Kaufmann was an HR officer with AlliedSignal, he sat in on all division planning sessions to forge the link between business strategy and talent. This link does not happen in most companies today: Only 7 percent of the managers we surveyed strongly agreed that their companies "link business strategy to specific talent pool requirements."[11] This is an important new role for HR.
- *Serve as the thought leader in understanding what it takes to attract great talent.* The HR officer should be—as Greg Summe

in talent-building actions. That's because most companies don't look at such expenditures as investments. Leaders with a talent mindset, however, do invest in new hires, higher salaries, relocation packages, separation packages, signing bonuses, stock options, and other elements that can help build a strong talent pool.

When it comes to attracting and retaining top talent, don't be recently told his fifty senior HR officers—"the barometer of the organization, understanding morale, recruiting and retention trends, as well as other people issues." The HR officer should help the management team clarify and strengthen the company's attractiveness to talent—and should monitor how satisfied managers are through surveys and informal discussions. With this knowledge, they can help leaders develop and execute explicit strategies for attracting and retaining talent.

- *Facilitate the talent review and action plans.* HR leaders should help facilitate the talent review process and then be the conscience of each unit to nudge and help all leaders execute the many actions they agreed to. This role includes having a nose for weak spots (people, structures, processes, and culture) and being comfortable in pushing senior leaders to deal proactively with those weak spots.

- *Become the architect of the development strategy for the top 50 to 100 managers.* This will require good assessment skills, good listening skills, candor, and insight. From our research, we know most organizations are not effective at using job assignments to drive development. HR should be the advisor to all leaders on their options and best choices for all job openings.

To perform this strategic role well, the HR leader will have to ensure that the less strategic technical functions of compensation administration, benefits, relocation, and so on are either delegated to superb technical specialists or outsourced.

Today, many more CFOs than HR leaders are on division management teams or corporate executive committees. Now that talent is so crucial to competitive success, look for that to change. Talent is the job of line leaders but they will need and welcome a strategic partnership with outstanding HR executives.

constrained by the old compensation rules. When necessary, break or rewrite the rules to bring in the right outsiders, retain A players, and invest in enough talent for growth. SunTrust Banks is an interesting case to learn from.

In 1995, the revenues at SunTrust Banks, the Atlanta-based diversified financial services company, were growing at about 4 percent per year. However, to boost shareholders' return to 15 percent a year, the company knew it would have to increase revenue of its existing businesses from 4 percent to 10 percent. SunTrust worked on four levers to boost its growth: new and better products, new channels, better and lower cost operations, and "more and better people." Once SunTrust achieved this goal, Phil Humann, the CEO, was convinced that by far the biggest driver of the growth was the addition of more people and the upgrade to higher performers. Talented people are, after all, the basis for better products, new channels, and better operations.

As part of its new emphasis on talent, SunTrust set out to hire 600 new relationship managers within their twenty-four banks throughout the South. That required money for signing bonuses and guaranteed bonuses, and it required a lot of time from hundreds of leaders to recruit and assimilate talent. To encourage the local bank presidents to make this investment right away, the corporate center absorbed the first year's total compensation and hiring expenses for the new hires.

In addition, the heads of the twenty-four banks decided they had to deal with low performers in key leadership positions in their six lines of business. Through assessment and forced rankings, they found that low-performing managers held about 20 percent of the 200 key line-of-business positions in those banks. Some of the low performers raised their game; they just hadn't been challenged with tough goals, candid feedback, and clear upside and downside consequences in the past. Others were transferred to incentive-based sales roles, and the rest were offered packages for early retirement.

The cost of hiring 600 new people and paying for the separation of others totaled about $50 million. For a company earning $800 million a year after tax, that amounted to a substantial 4 percent of pre-tax earnings. However, it paid off. In the first year, SunTrust raised its growth rate from 4 percent to 10 percent. Between 1996 and 1999, it held that growth rate at about 9 percent per year. This increased growth rate resulted in a 15 percent higher P/E ratio than its peers in 1997 and 1998, which allowed SunTrust to make the major acquisition of Crestar Bank in 1999.

Most companies and leaders appear reluctant to invest in talent. Yet our studies suggest that highly talented managers are 50 percent to 130 percent more productive than average- and low-performing managers.[12] Thus, the return on spending is typically substantial. Companies often spend millions on moderately high-risk capital projects with four- to five-year paybacks, yet balk at spending a fraction of that on more and better people. As you ponder this issue, think about the compelling impact talent-building has had at The Limited, PerkinElmer, and SunTrust Banks.

Sixth, leaders should hold themselves and their managers accountable for the strength of the talent pools they build

Almost all of the corporate officers we surveyed told us that "managers should be held accountable for the strength of their talent pool" (see figure 2-3). That makes a lot of sense. But only a few of them said their company actually does so. This is one of the most startling insights from our four years of research.

Figure 2-3 Should Line Managers Be Accountable for the Strength of the Talent Pool They Build?

% of corporate officers who think it's very important and % who strongly agree that their companies actually do this

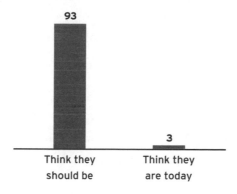

Source: McKinsey & Company's War for Talent 2000 Survey

Why aren't companies holding managers accountable for talent? You might argue that talent management is too difficult to measure, or that companies tend to consider talent as an input, whereas performance is gauged by output—growth and profits. These are fair points, but are you really comfortable not holding anyone accountable for the strength of the talent pool, especially when competitive advantage and economic value are demonstrably linked to your ability to build a strong talent pool?

Twenty years ago, most companies knew that productivity, quality, and customer satisfaction were important. However, few companies were able to measure them, and few managers, if any, were held accountable for them. It was only after companies learned how to measure these factors that they became critical business yardsticks.

Similarly, now is the time to hold ourselves accountable for the strength of our talent pools. Accountability can and should be the linchpin. But how?

Each unit—be it a store, research lab, sales force, or division—should set three to six specific talent pool strengthening objectives for the coming year. Obviously, each unit's objectives will change from year to year and setting these objectives will require judgment. The judgments brought to bear should involve several people in the unit and several people above the unit. Measuring success will require judgment, too. It will require ongoing discussions and calibrations about how effectively the talent pool is being built. These conversations are precisely what is *not* happening in any systematic, comprehensive, probing way in companies today—but should be. Accountability is the linchpin to deeply instilling a talent mindset and making talent management every leader's job.

———————

These six actions will not be easy; they will take 30 percent to 50 percent of your time. You might be wondering, "How can I make room for that kind of time commitment? I already have ten top three priorities." First, in every meeting, every phone call, and on every trip, talk about the talent aspects of the issue at hand. Bring every discussion back to the action plan that came out of the talent review process. Talent is a topic that should come up ten to twelve times per day as a part of conducting business. Second, let talent issues crowd out less important topics—delegate some of the other things you do to the talented managers working with you.

Simply stated, what is a better use of your time? Chairing budget meetings? Visiting customers? Picking sweaters? Couldn't you delegate some of those things if you had better people around you? For every hour you spend strengthening your team or helping your people strengthen their teams, think of the many hours of leverage you get.

Not Some Optional Deal

Kevin Sharer, CEO of Amgen, spends a lot of his time and attention on talent management. He believes that building a strong talent pipeline is as critical to his company's success as building a vibrant product pipeline. In fact, he believes the product pipeline and talent pipeline are directly linked, and that these are Amgen's two top priorities.

To build the talent pipeline, Sharer says, "I have tried to convince our top managers that if they believe people and people processes are HR's responsibility, they have totally missed the point. People are every manager's responsibility. That's the only way we will strengthen our talent pipeline."

Amgen, with a market cap of about $70 billion, makes two of the world's blockbuster biotech drugs: Epogen, used to combat anemia in kidney dialysis patients, and Neupogen, used to fight chemotherapy-induced infections in cancer patients. Under Sharer's leadership, the team at the top has hammered out a vision to become "the best human therapeutics company in the world." This requires competing with the bigger players—Merck, Pfizer, Johnson & Johnson, and others. It also requires a vast pipeline of new drugs. The pipeline now includes promising drugs to treat anemia, rheumatoid arthritis, and prostate cancer, but more products are required. Commercializing these products requires world-class skills in product development, marketing, international operations, alliance building, patent protection, and communications.

To build the talent pipeline, Sharer has put in place a talent review process for the company's top 500 managers, a process that he uses to identify stars for development and further responsibility. Important talent gaps in research, sales, marketing, planning, and HR have also been identified. To fill these gaps, several dozen highly talented outsiders have been brought into the top 100. Sharer has also begun to aggressively develop the high-potential talent that already existed in the company.

When we asked Sharer how confident he was that he could convince leaders, managers, and scientists to embrace a talent mindset—and make talent their job—he responded, "We're making good progress. When you're working with me, strengthening your talent pool is not some optional deal."

Check Your Talent Mindset

As you reflect on the actions of these leaders, ask yourself what you believe about the role of talent in your business and how talent management fits into your concept of your job:

- Do you believe having better people is how you will win in your business?

- Do you believe strengthening your talent pool is a crucial part of *your* job?

- Do you convince all your managers to make talent a crucial part of *their* jobs?

- Have you established a gold standard for talent in your organization that is widely understood and drives people decisions?

- Are you deeply involved in key people decisions two and three levels below you? Do you probe, help, and challenge?

- Do you personally drive a talent review process in each unit reporting to you that results in a robust agenda for substantially strengthening each unit's talent pool? Do you follow up continuously on each unit's plan?

- To instill a talent mindset in others, do you model great talent management and talk to your people about talent frequently?

- Have you demonstrated a willingness to invest real money in talent?

- Are you holding each of your leaders (and yourself) accountable for three to six highly specific and measurable actions to strengthen their talent pool over the coming year?

The answers to these questions must be an unequivocal "yes." Your company's performance is at stake. Embrace a talent mindset and help ensure that your company has the talent it needs to win in the marketplace.

3

CRAFT A WINNING
EMPLOYEE VALUE
PROPOSITION

A generation ago, a career was a means to an end—bread on the table, a roof over your family's head, and status someday as a manager in a large, respected company. You joined the company, did the job you were assigned, and climbed the corporate ladder at a slow and deliberate pace. Your career and pay didn't peak until you were in your fifties or early sixties.

Today, a career is a drastically different proposition. Talented people want the big money and all the perks. More important, though, they want to feel passionate about their work, excited by their jobs, enriched by their career opportunities, uplifted by the company's leaders, assured by the depth of its management, and inspired by its sense of mission. They'll work hard but they want to be fulfilled. If they're not fulfilled, they'll be inclined to leave. Highly talented managers have lots of attractive options to choose from. They understand how much value they can create. For these reasons, the "price" of talent—in financial and nonfinancial terms—has gone up.

A good example of a company that understands the need to meet these higher expectations is DoubleClick, the Internet advertising pioneer. When Dwight Merriman and Kevin O'Connor started the company in 1996, they built a value proposition for employees based not only on all the "new economy" bells and whistles—everything from an espresso bar in the lobby to free salsa lessons—but, more important, on the excitement of pioneering a new era in Internet advertising.

In addition, the value proposition they built gave employees the opportunity to control and shape their own careers. Merriman and O'Connor encouraged their people to switch jobs within the company, learn new skills, and take risks. For Chip Scovic, DoubleClick's proposition was enough to encourage him to drop out of a six-year law career to join the company. Though DoubleClick didn't have an immediate job for Scovic, they made him a "free agent" and moved him to San Francisco, where he now heads up some of the company's largest account teams for technical-solutions publishers. Reflecting on the opportunities at DoubleClick, he comments, "I have been able to take my career anywhere I've wanted."

At DoubleClick, employees are given a high degree of autonomy over the work they do. In return, the company expects a high degree of entrepreneurial drive—and results. For people at all levels, salary raises and bonuses are based on business results and their own performance. And there's downside risk, too: Those who don't deliver innovative thinking, great numbers, and strong people leadership might well be demoted or terminated. CEO Kevin Ryan expects that a number of low performers will be asked to leave each year.

"I judge my people on two people leadership questions," explains Ryan. "Are the people in their group happy working for them? And do they bring in great people? If managers can't help us attract and retain the best people, then they aren't doing a good job. Their compensation and bonus will directly reflect their ability to do this."

But the real test of DoubleClick's employee value proposition came with the Nasdaq drop that began in the spring of 2000. Along with the other dot-coms, DoubleClick's stock plummeted more than 80 percent, sending its employees' stock options underwater. To some observers, even the future of Internet advertising looked uncertain.

Remarkably, though, while many dot-coms lost many of their

best employees in the downturn, DoubleClick didn't lose any of its top 100 people. This wasn't because of the options, the coffee bar, or the salsa lessons. It was because DoubleClick had an employee value proposition that was compelling, exciting, and in tune with what its people wanted from their careers. To the extent that DoubleClick prospers in the future, it will be due in some significant measure to its robust employee value proposition and the strong talent pool that it has built as a result. A winning employee value proposition, in fact, is what all companies need to attract and hold on to their best employees, in good times and in bad.

What Is an Employee Value Proposition?

An employee value proposition (EVP) is the holistic sum of everything people experience and receive while they are part of a company—everything from the intrinsic satisfaction of the work to the environment, leadership, colleagues, compensation, and more. It's about how well the company fulfills people's needs, their expectations, and even their dreams. A strong EVP attracts great people like flowers attract bees. A strong EVP excites people so that they recommit daily to give their best—so that they are jazzed and feeling passionate about their work and their company.

The employee value proposition is not the fancy words in the recruiting brochure or the inspirational posters hanging on the conference room walls, nor is it a loose collection of benefits. It is what people really experience in the company, day by day.

An *employee* value proposition is similar to a *customer* value proposition. For more than a century, marketers have been consciously crafting customer value propositions. In the late 1800s, for instance, soap makers were still peddling their bars and powders as mere soap, at most with a pretty box to attract the customer's attention. Then someone began to think about what the customer really wanted when buying soap: how well it cleaned, how it smelled, how it affected their skin, how it was packaged, how it made them feel about what they were doing for their families when they used it, and of course, what it cost.[1]

Manufacturers started to figure out which attributes of their product were superior to the competitors' products and which were inferior. They segmented the customer pool to identify who would be most attracted to the value proposition of their product. Then they decided which aspects of their product to change, based on a rigorous analysis of what would really make a difference in buyers' behavior. In short, they began to think strategically about their customer value proposition, and they began to shape their products and business strategy accordingly. This may be conventional wisdom now, but at the time it was revolutionary.

Now, with companies competing hard to win the war for talent, they have to start applying the same kind of marketing thinking to attracting and retaining employees. Your company needs a strong employee value proposition—a compelling answer to the question, "Why would a highly talented person choose to work here?"

In this chapter, we will describe the critical elements that managers look for when they choose a company, and we describe how some companies deliver superbly on those demands. We show you that the core EVP elements are a fundamental part of the organization, and therefore not easily changed. Finally, we describe what makes up a winning EVP and how you can use marketing techniques to help your company build one.

What Managers Are Looking For

What do talented managers look for when deciding which company to join? We asked them how important various items are when making those decisions. Figure 3-1 shows that some items are considered critical by a large number of managers while others are not. We also asked managers how well their current company delivers on those items. The bold items in figure 3-1 are the ones that have a strong causal relationship with the overall level of satisfaction reported.[2] In figure 3-2 we show just how powerfully the key elements of the EVP affect managers' satisfaction levels.

Figure 3-1 What Managers Are Looking For

% of respondents who rate the item critical in their decision of which company to join and stay with

EXCITING WORK

✓ **Interesting, challenging work**	**59%**
✓ **Work I feel passionate about**	**45%**
I am listened to and can impact decisions	41%
Take initiative and own success	40%
Have impact in the company	35%
Freedom and autonomy	31%
Participate in strategic directions	22%
Encouraged to innovate	22%

DEVELOPMENT

✓ **Career advancement opportunities**	**37%**
✓ **Long-term commitment to me**	**35%**
✓ **Build skills to boost career**	**35%**
✓ Sr. managers committed to me	30%
✓ **High performers promoted**	**28%**
Frequent feedback	17%
Receive helpful mentoring	16%
Ongoing training	14%

LIFESTYLE

Can meet my personal/family commitments	51%
Live in appealing city/region	34%
Reasonable work pace	11%
Flexibility of when/where I work	9%

GREAT COMPANY

✓ **Company is well managed**	**48%**
✓ **Good relations with my boss**	**43%**
✓ **I like the culture and values**	**39%**
✓ **I trust senior management**	**38%**
Not hampered by bureaucracy	30%
✓ **A boss I admire**	**26%**
Exciting, interesting industry	24%
Industry has growth prospects	22%
Products make a difference	21%
Company is a strong performer	21%
People are high performers	19%
Company's reputation	17%
Camaraderie with colleagues	13%
Contribution beyond the bottom line	9%
People with diverse backgrounds	8%
Positive impact on society	6%

WEALTH AND REWARDS

✓ **Recognized, rewarded for my individual contribution**	**39%**
✓ **Substantial wealth creation opportunity**	**36%**
✓ **High performers paid more**	**31%**
✓ **Annual cash comp is high**	**26%**

✓ **Bolded** = items that make up the elements that have a strong causal relationship with satisfaction

Source: McKinsey & Company's War for Talent 2000 Survey, middle and senior managers

Figure 3-2 Effect of Key Elements on Satisfaction

% of respondents satisfied with current employer

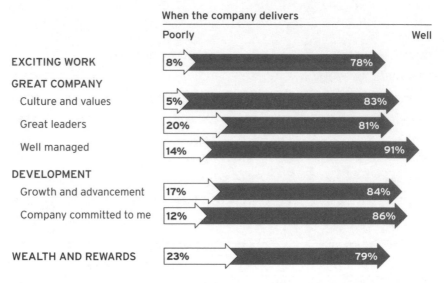

When the company delivers

	Poorly	Well
EXCITING WORK	8%	78%
GREAT COMPANY		
Culture and values	5%	83%
Great leaders	20%	81%
Well managed	14%	91%
DEVELOPMENT		
Growth and advancement	17%	84%
Company committed to me	12%	86%
WEALTH AND REWARDS	23%	79%

Source: McKinsey & Company's War for Talent 2000 Survey, middle and senior managers

In our surveys, managers told us they want exciting, challenging jobs and they want to feel passionate about their work. They want to be inspired by the mission of the company, they want to launch new businesses and products, and they want big jobs that provide the opportunity to stretch.

Second, the surveys reveal that managers want to work for great companies. They look for well-managed firms that have great leaders and for cultures that emphasize a performance orientation and an open, trusting environment.

Third, we learned that people are looking for wealth-creation opportunities and they want their individual contribution recognized in their pay. Money is important, but this is about more than just the tangible value of the money. It's also about psychic gratification.

Fourth, managers told us they want the company to help them develop their skills. This is particularly important today, as people realize that their only career security lies in the collection of skills and experiences that they bring to the job market.

The Old Expectations	The New Expectations
Big budget and large staff	New challenges and exciting businesses
Traditional corporate hierarchy	Flat, fluid, flexible organization
Thirty-year horizon, good salary and retirement package	Five-year horizon, wealth linked to value created
Steadily up the corporate ladder	Jumping from one rock face to another

Finally, managers indicated they wanted a job that would allow them to meet their personal and family commitments.

EVP Elements Are a Fundamental Part of the Company

To create a compelling employee value proposition, a company must provide the core elements that managers look for—exciting work, a great company, attractive compensation, and opportunities to develop. A few more perks, casual dress, or more generous health plans won't make the difference between a weak EVP and a strong one. If you want to substantially strengthen your company's EVP, be prepared to change things as fundamental as the business strategy, the organization structure, the culture, and even the caliber of leaders in the organization.

Exciting work to feel passionate about

A great EVP starts with interesting, challenging work that people can feel passionate about. For some companies, that mandate seems simple to fulfill. If you are the Virgin Group, for instance, you have charismatic CEO Richard Branson dreaming up all kinds of exciting ventures—from Virgin Atlantic Airways, to Virgin Megastores, to Virgin Mobile, and Virgin Direct (financial services). If you are America

Online, you are at the cutting edge of the Internet, with Time Warner as your new playground. These companies have excitement and challenge embedded in their business and their brands.

Amgen is another company whose business is inherently exciting to people. Amgen began in 1980, on the cusp of the biotechnology revolution. Two of Amgen's drugs have been blockbusters, with $3 billion in sales between them. From a start-up, Amgen grew into the biggest biotech firm in the world.

The appeal of Amgen's EVP goes even deeper than that, however. Amgen's two biggest drugs, Epogen and Neupogen, help dialysis patients and cancer patients better handle the effects of their treatments. For this reason, the company's tacit motto is goose-pimply: "We defeat death."

Executive Vice President Dennis Fenton recalls the day when that message hit home. "We were trying to determine what drew people to the company and what kept them here," he says. "We considered our top-ten market cap, being the franchise leader in oncology, and things like that. And I said, 'You know, that's not what gets most of the people I know coming to Amgen. What draws them is the concept that we're helping people live longer—we're defeating death.'"

For Amgen employees, that message strikes home and makes Amgen a special place to work. "I was manning the Amgen booth at a medical conference last weekend," explains Catherine Buck, Director of Operations Projects in Boulder, Colorado. "There was a young man who had cancer. He had his little kids with him. He was using Neupogen. He came up to me in the booth and said, 'In my family, we call this liquid gold.'"

Amgen, Virgin, and AOL Time Warner have excitement and meaning embedded in their business. But what about other companies? How do you attract employees to work that is considerably less glamorous or seemingly less exciting and interesting?

The answer: You have to *make* your business and jobs exciting. Innovate faster than anyone else, start new businesses, launch new products. Create a mission that is inspiring. Challenge yourself and your employees to transform your business.

Enron did this and more. Enron wasn't born in an exciting industry. It was formed in 1985, when Houston Natural Gas merged with InterNorth, a natural gas company based in Omaha, Nebraska. In 1990 Jeff Skilling, a former consultant, and Gene Humphrey, who was president of Enron's finance corporation, started a new division of Enron called Enron Capital and Trade. Its purpose was to build a business around trading natural gas, something that had never been done before.

That was the beginning of a whole new business. From a stodgy gas pipeline firm, the company has evolved into a world-class risk management player—parlaying those skills into a $55 billion empire. Now Enron trades gas, electricity, paper, minerals, water, and even broadband capacity. The payoff has been a soaring stock price and a capitalization that has reached the third highest level in the United States.

But there's more. Enron also created a new EVP for itself as a company that thrives on deal-making, the chance to do something big, the promise of turning commodity markets upside down, and— not incidentally—the possibility of making a lot of money at the same time. "You'll have the opportunity to completely change the way business is done in many industries," Kevin Hannon, head of Enron's new broadband unit tells his eager recruits. "You'll be an architect designing how those markets are created and how they are grown."

Enron's EVP was built to attract the kind of talent the company needed. Enron CEO Jeff Skilling knew he would need a different kind of person than those recruited for the pipeline business. He would need to convince traders with experience at the best commodity exchanges and investment banks to join his team. So strong was Skilling's recognition of this challenge that he agreed to join Enron only on the condition that he would have complete freedom to hire whomever he needed and manage them in a different way. "We could never have successfully launched Enron Capital and Trade had we not attracted different kinds of people and offered a different kind of value proposition," Skilling remarks. "It was a central part of the concept of the new division."

In creating this new EVP, Skilling established an internal job market, one in which people could move quickly to the business units and jobs in which they had the most interest and in which they found the greatest challenge. Internal poaching was encouraged and no one was allowed to hold people back from a move.

When Enron launched its Global Broadband unit, for instance, Kevin Hannon, who had been the COO of Enron North America, jumped over to start the new business. Needing fifty people for the new unit, he launched "Project Quick Hire," inviting 100 top performers from around the company to the Houston Hyatt for a day-long meeting. There, he presented his business plan to his colleagues. After the briefings, "recruiters" were posted outside the banquet hall with sign-up sheets. Hannon had his fifty top performers for the broadband unit by the end of the week—and his peers had fifty holes to fill.

This system gives people the chance to move at a very fast pace. David Delainey, CEO of Enron's North American unit, provides an example. When Delainey joined Enron, he was initially attracted by the high upside that Enron promised. And besides, he thought, if the job didn't work out, he could always go back to his marketing job with Shell Oil in Calgary. He didn't have to worry, however; ever since joining Enron, his career path has gone straight up: From 1994 to 1997 he was manager of Enron's gas marketing business in Canada. He next moved to Houston to run Enron's Eastern U.S. origination business. Within a year of his move he was promoted to run the origination business for the entire United States. At the beginning of 1999, Delainey was the Chief Commercial Officer for North America, and by the end of the year he was its CEO. When he made CEO of North America, incidentally, Delainey was just thirty-four years old.

"We base our business model on people's desire to try new challenges and achieve success," Skilling explains. "I don't want anyone sitting in the same position for five years and getting bored. Fluid movement is absolutely necessary in our company. And the type of people we hire enforces that. Not only does this system help the excitement level for each manager, it shapes Enron's business in the direction that its managers find most exciting."

There are limits to where Enron may go, of course, but as Skilling notes, "If lots of people are flocking to a new business unit, that's a good sign that the opportunity is a good one," he explains. "If a business unit can't attract people very easily, that's a good sign that it's a business Enron shouldn't be in."

Few companies will be able to achieve the excitement extravaganza that Enron has in its remarkable business transformation, but many could apply some of the principles.

When shaping your business strategy, think about guiding the company in a direction that would be exciting to highly talented people. Elevate the mission of the company to something that inspires passion. Consider structuring the organization in a way that creates more expansive and interesting roles for people. Create jobs that have elbow room and head room; give people as much autonomy and responsibility as possible. Where possible, create more jobs with profit and loss responsibility and more cross-functional teams so people can get their arms around a business.

Great company, great culture, great leaders

Beyond the work that they are doing, managers want to be a part of a great company. They want to like the culture and values, feel they are part of a well managed company, and have leaders who inspire them.

Different people prefer different kinds of corporate cultures. However, there are two aspects of culture that nearly all managers are looking for: a strong performance orientation and an open, trusting environment.

Figure 3-3 shows the percentage of managers who like the culture of their companies.[3] Companies that have both a performance orientation (which includes inspiring mission, stretch goals, accountability for results, and tight performance systems) and an open, trusting environment have more managers satisfied with the culture. It's easy to think that these two cultural characteristics are mutually exclusive, but they are not. In fact, they are a powerful combination.[4]

Figure 3-3   People Want Both Cultural Dimensions

% of respondents who like their company's culture

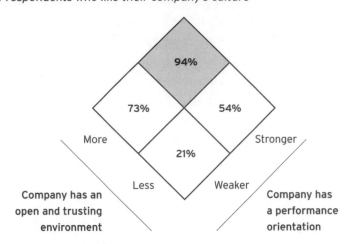

Source: McKinsey & Company's War for Talent 2000 Survey, middle and senior managers

In addition to a great culture, people are looking for leaders who inspire and challenge them. They want their immediate bosses, in addition to the CEO, to be good leaders. Great leadership is even more important to members of Generation X than it is to older executives. In our survey, Gen-Xers rated "good relationship with my boss" third in their list of elements that drive their career decisions, just behind interesting work and being able to meet their family and personal commitments.[5] In their relationships with their bosses, Gen-Xers want a high degree of autonomy, and they want to be coached.

Terrific leadership and a great culture can be a central part of a winning EVP, as Synovus Financial Corp. has discovered. When *Fortune*'s "100 Best Companies to Work For" issue came out in 1999, many readers were surprised at the company that topped the list. It wasn't a household name. In fact, even the CEO of the company was surprised when he got the news. He knew his company had worked hard on its culture and leadership for several years, but he truly thought they had a long way to go.

That company is Synovus Financial Corp., a medium-sized financial services firm headquartered in Columbus, Georgia, ninety miles south of Atlanta. Two years prior to the company's topping the *Fortune* list, the leaders of the organization gathered for their weekly meeting. They had just completed two decades of blistering growth. Toward the end of the hour-long meeting, one bold individual took the floor and posed a question to the executive officers. They didn't know at the time that that question would fundamentally change the company's EVP.

The individual, a midlevel investment banker, began by praising the company: "Synovus has grown exponentially over the last century and especially in the last two decades. We've expanded into new businesses, new regions, and new technology. We now have a diverse family of 10,000 employees and profits are up." Pausing for a moment to clear his throat, he then posed, "But in light of all of our business success, have we lost sight of our people?" The room went silent. The sentiment behind his question was not lost on anyone and all present agreed: The company must nurture its caring spirit, the very hallmark it was founded on.

Then began the monumental task of fortifying their culture. Jimmy Blanchard, the company's CEO, reports, "We all agreed on a mission: to create a workplace where every person who works here knows someone gives a darn about them; a workplace free of harassment, manipulation, secretiveness, jerking around; an absence of 'saluting the flag and kicking the dog' attitudes." Over time they came to call the culture they aspired to create "A Culture of the Heart."

After many rounds of companywide surveys and numerous hard-pushing conversations, Blanchard and his team codified their expectations of all leaders going forward. To be a successful leader at Synovus now, one must: (1) Live the Values—at work, home, and in the community you must exemplify qualities of integrity, character, and principle; (2) Share the Vision—stand up and tell your story to inspire others to greatness; (3) Make Others Successful—send your people out to higher callings than you have experienced; and (4)

Manage the Business—execute on these points while performing the best banking practices and earning high returns for shareholders.

For the first time in the company's 113-year history, the leaders of Synovus put pen to paper on culture issues. They wanted it in writing that success at Synovus can only be achieved through the unconditional support of the Culture of the Heart—the realization that a manager's most important role is to serve, grow, and inspire his or her people—with no exceptions.

With a vision on paper, Synovus needed to bring it to life. They started by expecting—indeed requiring—every senior leader and every manager to visibly and actively behave in ways that reinforce the values. Then they instituted processes to reinforce the leadership behaviors and established forums to encourage discussion, identify issues, and generate solutions. These included a culture-focused orientation program; a Cultural Trust Committee, which meets monthly for three or four hours to discuss issues regarding the Culture of the Heart; Ask-the-CEO town-hall meetings open to all employees; and Right Steps, a review process that separates leadership reviews from personal performance reviews.

Although the Culture of the Heart and the programs to make it happen sound soft, they have a hard edge to them as well. The values are explicitly woven into the performance evaluation process. Leaders in the top 200 are evaluated on how inspirational and effective they are as leaders, how they get results, and how they look after their people. About 30 of the top 200 managers have been eased out of the company for not living the Culture of the Heart.

Reflecting on the last four years and their 2001 placement at number eight on *Fortune*'s coveted list, Blanchard confides, "Beyond the programs we've instituted, I don't know of a meeting since 1996 where we haven't talked about personally developing everyone. I'm now a true believer that having a great culture is essential to growing a profitable company."

Blanchard can say this with some confidence: Synovus's market capitalization grew from $2.2 billion to $8 billion over these four years.

Wealth and rewards

Few questions are as elusive as what money means, what it's worth, and how much of one's life one should spend in its pursuit. Michael Lewis, author of *Liar's Poker* and *The New New Thing* noted, "A person who missed out on the Wall Street bonanza could say to himself, 'Well, I may not be rich, but at least I'm not a jerk.' A person who has missed out on the Internet Boom is left with no such consoling thought. Either you are rich or you are a chump. People no longer feel guilty for making a lot of money. They feel guilty for not making a lot of money."[6]

The economic downturn has changed those expectations, of course, but the 1990s boom has left its mark. In the past, people were paid according to the desk they sat at. When they moved up a pay grade, their salary rose to that specified point. Today, talented managers expect to make a lot of money, and they want it sooner rather than later. The dot-com gold rush, although it didn't last long, left an indelible image on the minds of many people.

The price of talent is indeed going up. Starting compensation for M.B.A. students at the top twenty-five schools has gone up 36 percent to $127,000 in the last four years.[7] CEO compensation went up tenfold in the last ten years to an average of $12.4 million.[8] Many consulting firms, investment banks, and law firms increased compensation 30 percent to 50 percent in the last few years of the 1990s.

We don't think the higher levels of managerial compensation will go away. Yes, the bull market and the dot-com craze drove some of the increase, but much of it was driven by the rising value of talent, by greater expectations of talented managers, and by a growing awareness on the part of managers that their contributions directly drive the performance of the company.

For all these reasons and more, compensation is critical to attracting and keeping managers. It's not just the absolute amount of compensation that matters, though. In our survey, reward and recognition for high individual performance was rated important by more managers than the overall amount of cash or wealth they are paid (see figure 3-1).

We asked the survey respondents if they were likely to leave their company in the near future and why. "Insufficient reward or recognition" was one of the top four reasons.[9] There are many ways companies can recognize the contributions managers make, but money is an important one. Many managers view money as a scorecard for how well they are performing and how much the company values their talent.

While it takes more than money to build a winning EVP, if you don't stay competitive with the market price for the best managerial talent, you'll have a hard time building a winning EVP. As Ed Lawler pointed out in *Rewarding Excellence*, it is rare that people accept the lowest paying job option.[10] Some companies will choose to make superior compensation a central part of their value proposition to talent by paying more than competitors. Others will choose to pay competitively, but not above the going rate. Don't let compensation slip much below the going rate, however, because that can be a significant handicap in your EVP.

Companies are also going to have to change their compensation systems so that they can pay the best performers significantly more than average performers. Traditional compensation systems are designed to pay people doing the same jobs the same amount of money. The new systems should pay people according to the amount

Old Pay Philosophy	New Pay Philosophy
Pay for the job	Pay for the person and for performance
Job scope and seniority drive pay	Value creation drives pay
Pay what others in the company get (internal equity)	Pay what the individual could get elsewhere (market equity)
Set a range and hire within it	Break the compensation rules to hire the right candidate

of value they create. This will allow companies to pay top performers what they are worth in the market without raising compensation levels across the board for everyone. This pay-for-the-person approach is a significant departure for most companies. As companies work through these new compensation philosophies, there is bound to be friction. However, it will ultimately be easier for those that do make the transition to attract and retain great talent.

Enron is a good example of a company that has broken the link between compensation and particular jobs. At Enron, there are four main "levels" of managers in the company: vice president, managing director, business unit CEO/COO, and office of the chairman. Unlike most titles, the ones at Enron are portable—they travel with the individual. Even if the individual takes on another job or task, his or her title remains the same.

"Your title is not your job; your job is not your title," explains Enron CEO Jeff Skilling. "If you are a vice president of Enron, then you are a vice president regardless of what you do. So, if you want to go to Japan and start an office, and for a couple of months that means you are sweeping the floors, you're still a vice president of Enron and you'll be compensated accordingly."

Within these broad levels, managers at Enron are paid according to their performance and contribution to the company. In addition to being paid for the performance of their business unit and the overall performance of the company, managers receive a sizable portion of their pay based on their own individual performance. Once a year, all employees are force-ranked and cross-calibrated within their peer group. Enron calls this talent review process the Performance Review Committee. An employee ranking "superior" on a six-point scale can receive as much as 30 percent of their salary in cash bonuses and 50 percent in long-term equity incentives. Those ranking "satisfactory" receive a small bonus and no options. If you receive a ranking of "has issues" or "needs improvement," you'll see nothing more than your salary that year.

"It's demoralizing for some to be working their tails off and producing results, when others aren't and they're all getting paid the same amount," explains Cindy Olson, Enron's HR director. "That is never going to inspire the innovative thinking that we need. I would rather everyone's pay reflect the direct contribution they are making to the organization than everyone receive the same pay."

Whereas Enron's pay structure has a large component that is driven by individual performance, some companies may choose to base the incentive pay entirely on team performance. These companies, however, will still need a salary structure that allows them to pay wide differences in salary levels, so they can still pay the most capable people significantly more in total compensation. To be successful, the system must ensure individuals are paid commensurate with their contribution and their worth in the market.[11]

Growth and development

In today's uncertain market, people have learned that security no longer rests in the corporate nest egg, but in their own skills. For that reason, talented people are drawn to companies that will help them develop new skills, knowledge, and experiences.

Gen-X managers, in particular, value development. Throughout the 1980s, they watched as their parents were laid off. They know that the paternalistic corporation is no longer a reality. Beyond that, Gen-Xers are voracious learners. They grew up with the fast, self-paced learning of video games, computers, and the Internet. They were educated in schools that emphasized problem solving over rote memorization.[12]

At work, Gen-Xers love to learn new things. They crave frequent feedback and mentoring. Bill Rogers discovered this with his people at SunTrust Banks: "Young managers today want clear goals for the week on Monday, some feedback on Wednesday, and a performance review on Friday." If young managers don't get the kind of career development and learning they crave, they will simply go elsewhere to get it.

Arrow Electronics, the world's largest distributor of electronic components and computer products, has made developing its people a central part of its EVP. It had to. Over the past thirty years Arrow has grown 30 percent per year. Between 1990 and 2000 the Melville, New York, company grew from less than $1 billion in revenues to $13 billion. It takes a lot of great talent to build an extraordinary company like that.

At first blush, however, Arrow seems an unlikely destination for the best recruits. The company is in the unglamorous business of distributing electronic components. It doesn't make anything, nor does it have exciting research labs. It doesn't have the brand sizzle of an Intel, Motorola, or Texas Instruments, some of the suppliers whose products Arrow distributes.

Somehow Arrow has managed to collect a group of 12,000 talented employees, some of them hailing from the best schools and M.B.A. programs in the world. How have they done it? First, they made their business attractive by becoming a global consolidator and by making the industry more efficient and professional. Second, they created a warm, caring culture that emphasizes merit and applauds the contributions of its people. Perhaps more than anything else, however, Arrow became a development greenhouse.

Arrow pulls all the development levers very effectively. Arrow's leaders deliberately and thoughtfully move people through developmental jobs. They offer ten-week sabbaticals to all employees after their first and second seven-year periods with the company. They put high-potential people into those vacated positions while the incumbents are on sabbatical. There is a well-conceived program to ensure maximum learning from that stretch experience.

Arrow also goes to great lengths to ensure that everyone in the company receives high-quality coaching, feedback, and mentoring. There is a training program on how to give performance evaluations that every manager must not only attend, but also pass before they can give an evaluation. Managers' coaching abilities are assessed on an ongoing basis using 360-degree feedback. Added to this mix is a world-class formal mentoring program (which you will read more about in chapter 5). To overcome the lack of glamour in its industry, Arrow used development, among other things, to craft a winning EVP.

Meeting personal and family commitments

Our survey data on lifestyle illustrate the complexity of this issue. Managers rated being able to meet personal and family commitments very high—the second highest item in the list of attributes they say affects their career decisions. Yet this item did not have a causal relationship with their self-reported satisfaction.

Our explanation of this apparent contradiction is that people have already accepted the lifestyle demands of their jobs. Interestingly, the more specific lifestyle elements—location, work pace, and flexibility—did not score very high. The managers in our survey did not seem to be saying that they want to work less or at a slower pace—they have, after all, opted into these very demanding and adrenaline-packed roles. We think they are saying that it is important to them to meet family commitments, but that they accept the trade-offs.

It is our belief that work–life balance will become an increasingly important objective when managers make their career choices. As Robert Reich pointed out in *The Future of Success*, our work lives have become increasingly pressured. The pace of business today and the 24/7 nature of communications methods make it hard for managers to get away from work.[13] Lifestyle issues will also start to play a larger role as women, Gen-Xers, and older workers make up a larger portion of the managerial ranks.

The human side

We would be remiss if we did not address the need for community and the sheer pleasure of colleagues in our discussion of EVP. After all, the very nature of managing means being plunked into the messy, marvelous path of human traffic. For so many people the most enjoyable part of work is the other people they work with. Colleagues can vex and peeve and disappoint us, but mostly, if we're lucky, they engage and stretch and inspire us. Each person at work has the opportunity to learn upward, downward, and laterally, and that is often the real reason we enter our offices each day.

Companies should realize that one of their most valuable offerings is the pleasure of other great colleagues and co-workers—teaching and learning from them, sharing with them, simply being with them. As the great South African playwright Athol Fugard said, "The only thing that ever matters in the world is what one person does or says to another person."

A Winning EVP Beats the Competition

A company's EVP is a holistic blend of many things—all the things, in fact that make up the company. Each company's EVP is different—as distinctive as a fingerprint. Although some companies may try to have a winning EVP on every dimension, few will achieve that. A winning EVP will have some towering strengths and a few weaknesses as well.

A winning EVP has to be tailored to appeal to the specific type of people the company is trying to attract. DoubleClick's EVP appeals to energetic Gen-Xers who love the Internet. Enron's EVP appeals to risk-loving, analytical, aggressive deal makers. Amgen's EVP appeals to people who love science and the notion of improving the quality of people's lives. An EVP cannot be all things to all people; those who love Enron's EVP, for instance, would probably dislike Amgen's, and vice versa.

A winning EVP also has to be better than the other options your target people are considering. Do you know who your talent competitors are? Is your EVP better than theirs? If you are a paper company looking to hire the very best managers with experience running paper mills, are you offering something better than the other paper companies? If you are Enron Capital and Trade, are you offering a better EVP than the investment banks? If you are a start-up, do you know who your competitors are—and what EVP will draw talent from them to you?

That was the challenge that Level 3 Communications faced a few years ago. In the late 1990s, CEO James Q. Crowe created Level 3 to build a continuously upgradeable, optical network using Internet Protocol (IP) technology. Crowe described the Level 3 technology as something way beyond herky-jerky videoconferencing: "We want to replicate the full experience of 'communication in the same room together' through the richness of all the human senses. There are revolutionary implications. When you can 'see' people so well, how can you go to bed knowing people are hungry? How can you wage war against your neighbor when you truly know your neighbor?"

By 1997, Crowe had raised $2.5 billion to back his new vision. But to implement his technological vision, Crowe and his leadership team knew they would have to attract a lot of great talent to come to work for them: risk-takers with IT and engineering expertise who were well-versed in the telecom industry. They also knew that there were dozens of other exciting high-tech start-ups out there all scrambling after the same talent that Level 3 needed.

Crowe and his partners met that challenge. Level 3's EVP became a powerful alchemy of inspiring mission, visionary leadership, entrepreneurial and performance-oriented culture, highly motivating compensation, and terrific location.

When we asked Linda Adams, Group VP of Human Resources, what the inspiring mission meant to her, she responded with a personal story. "Last summer I took my middle son, Alex, to the British Museum of Science and Technology. At the telecom exhibit we studied the chronology of innovations from the telegraph to fiber optic networks. As we were walking around the exhibit, I noticed on the wall pictures of visionaries in the field and I said to Alex, 'See right over here? At some point Jim Crowe and the Level 3 story will be there.'" Adams adds, "My own picture obviously won't be there, but I will know that I was a part of truly revolutionizing how people communicate."

Though there are many impressive leaders at Level 3, Crowe's particular style of leadership has been a magnet for talent. Don Gips, Group VP for Global Strategy, commented, "I've never met anybody smarter. Crowe is an amazingly broad thinker who can also understand things three levels down. He can explain complicated ideas in a way that people can easily grasp. And he's an incredibly decent human being."

The leadership team also understood that the right compensation package would be important. The package they crafted replicated the upside wealth creation opportunities offered by start-ups and the financial stability of established companies. It attracted risk takers and reinforced the performance orientation of the culture. While the salary was at the low end of the median, the options program offered high risk and high rewards.

Under the options program, all employees were granted options every quarter reflecting current stock prices, thereby creating new opportunities for wealth creation. The stock options had value when, and only when, Level 3's stock price outperformed the S&P 500 Index. When it did, there was a multiplier that significantly increased the value of the options. If the company did not outperform the S&P 500, the options were worthless.

Finally, the founding leaders set out to make location a distinctive strength. They hired a consulting firm to survey newly graduated and experienced engineers to determine what part of the country was most appealing to them. Based on that work, Crowe and his leadership team located the company in Broomfield, Colorado, just east of Boulder. They chose Broomfield for its quality of life, affordable cost of housing, and its accessible recreation facilities—the Rockies.

While the future success of many high-tech companies is uncertain, the power of the EVP created by Level 3 cannot be denied. Reflecting on that EVP, Adams enthused, "If I were to write down why I came here, I couldn't even dream it this good."

Keep Evolving the EVP

Even Level 3's strong EVP could lose its luster, though, if its talent competitors strengthen their EVPs, or if new talent competitors arrive on the scene. An EVP is not a static thing. Companies must keep evolving their EVPs to stay one step ahead of the competition. Just as food manufacturers change the flavors, sizes, and packaging of their products to reflect changing consumer needs, so must companies adjust their EVPs in response to marketplace threats.

Sometimes the changes to strengthen an EVP can occur gradually, but at other times they must happen swiftly. Consider the dramatic changes enacted by SunTrust Senior Vice President Mimi Breeden, who was in charge of SunTrust's sixty-seven Publix supermarket branches in Georgia.

In early 1998, two years after the first in-store branches were opened, Breeden's unit faced a major attrition crisis. Annual turnover rates were painfully high and nothing her team had tried seemed to last for long: 46 percent of all branch staff and 55 percent of the high performers were quitting annually. Breeden raised compensation, but to no avail. She bumped it up a second time, still no lasting results. So she decided to investigate deeper into the real causes of the turnover. She talked to the frontline staff and branch managers, walked around the branches, held focus groups, and did surveys.

Working on Sundays was a big complaint. Her people also didn't like the fact that their schedule sometimes changed unpredictably from week to week (often to fill gaps left by defecting workers). To address those problems, Breeden reviewed customer usage on weekends and decided to close all the branches on Sundays. She worked with her managers to institute a new scheduling system that would provide stability.

Breeden and her managers went even further, however. First, they encouraged employee input through 360-degree feedback on all senior managers. Second, they created development plans for each associate, which were reviewed monthly and updated semianually. As part of their effort to provide clearer career paths and advancement opportunities, they posted "opportunity alerts" to let people know about job openings in other parts of the bank.

Third, they provided certification training programs for field sales reps, assistant managers, and managers. Fourth, they nurtured top performers, making sure Breeden and her senior managers met with them and listened to their needs regularly. Fifth, they compensated aggressively for performance, including pay increases every six months instead of every year. And in some cases, they paid on-the-spot bonuses.

The changes hit the mark: Eighteen months later, the attrition rate of Breeden's in-store employees was down to 27 percent, the attrition of branch managers was down to 12 percent, and the attrition rate of A players was below 10 percent. "None of these things in itself was amazing," says Breeden, "but the breakthrough was that we did all of them *early* and *often*. I read a lot about young managers and found that they not only want a lot of challenge in their careers, they also want a lot of feedback and 'touch.'"

Breeden keeps a flat, palm-sized rock on her credenza to remind her of the retention lesson she has learned. "I keep this here because it makes me think of a story I once read about setting priorities." She explains, "Its message is that unless you focus on the 'big rocks' first, you'll never have room for them because the gravel and sand will always crowd them out. I use this image to focus on the time and attention we must invest to keep and motivate our good employees. If we spend our time wisely—put those big rocks first—then the performance of your business pretty much follows accordingly."

Furthermore, Breeden has learned how important the personal touch is in retaining valued employees. "A handwritten note thanking Eric for the great job he's done; an e-mail to Shannon acknowledging her great coaching skills; an impromptu lunch with Lauren," says Breeden. "What might surprise you is that I don't really think of myself as a classic 'people person.' I'm probably more of an analyst at heart. But my own 360-degree feedback suggested I could be more effective if I added a little 'high touch.' And when I think about it now, I do get energy from going out in the field and talking to people, seeing them perform their best and feeling valued by this bank. In fact, it makes it all worthwhile."

Think About It Like a Product or Market Strategy

Whether you are starting a new company, responding to an attrition crisis, or strengthening an already strong EVP, apply the same rigor to your EVP as you would to your customer value proposition. Adapt some of the diagnostic techniques that you use to develop a product or market strategy:

- Assess how strong your EVP is today. Measure attrition rates of high performers, new recruits, and other key groups. Analyze the acceptance rates of recruiting offers and the quality of new hires.

- Understand the needs of your target market. Conduct surveys and focus groups of current, prospective, and past employees to understand which EVP elements are most important to them and what drives their "buy" and "switch" decisions. Identify the segments that would be most attracted to your company's EVP.

- Understand how your EVP stacks up against the competition. Who are your talent competitors? What are the strengths and weaknesses of their EVPs compared to yours?

- Identify the strengths and vulnerabilities of your EVP. List the elements of your EVP that are towering strengths and those that are vulnerabilities.

- Decide which elements you are going to improve. Brainstorm all the ways you could strengthen your EVP and decide which the company will act on. The kinds of changes needed to substantially improve an EVP simply won't materialize unless you and other leaders accept and drive the change.

Just as products benefit from having a clear brand message, so does your EVP. Volvo makes products that are known for their safety. Volvo's brand communicates "a safe, reliable family car." Likewise, the essence of GE's EVP could be described as, "Be part of a world-class operation and become a world-class general manager."

A recruiting brand is the message that communicates your EVP to your target candidates. Because the message has to be short, it has to highlight the most compelling aspects of your EVP. Communicating the right recruiting brand helps you attract the kind of people you need for your organization. PeopleSoft, for example, advertised its recruiting brand in an award-winning, black-and-white ad campaign in *Fortune* magazine. Each ad featured an employee with an unusual hobby, prior career, or outside-of-work accomplishment (such as an Olympic gold medal swimmer and a former chicken and sheep farmer). The brand message was this: If you join us, you'll get to work with some of the most exciting, interesting, and talented people on the planet.[14]

Deliver on People's Dreams

Yes, talented managers expect a lot today. They also create a lot of value for their companies. Companies that want to attract and hold onto great talent have to deliver an EVP that satisfies people's expectations and out-competes their alternative options.

Substantially reshaping the employee value proposition requires rethinking the way you conduct your business, the way you advance your people, the way you structure jobs, and the way you measure performance. You may need to rethink the very culture of the organization. The changes may cut to the core of some of the most closely held traditions of the company.

This can be wrenching and will undoubtedly be met with some resistance, but don't let that deter you—the payoff can be enormous. Attracting and keeping highly talented people and bringing out the very best in your people will fuel your business.

Rest assured that even ordinary organizations can offer their people something extraordinary. They can deliver wonderfully satisfying careers and truly meet the aspirations of their people.

4

REBUILD YOUR
RECRUITING
STRATEGY

When Henry Ford decided to double the salaries at his High-
land Park, Michigan, assembly plant in 1914—from about
$2.50 to a fabulous $5 a day—the news made headlines in Detroit
and across the country. It was hardly necessary, though. Word had
already spread around town that the upstart car manufacturer
would be hiring at that wage.

Overnight, thousands of people began to line up at the factory
gates. At dawn they began filing through the hiring department,
hats in hand. On the other side of the desks were leagues of
employment agents, who interviewed the men and stamped their
papers. The lucky ones were chosen, and those not selected went
looking for work elsewhere.[1]

For generations, that's the way recruiting worked at most companies. The hiring department would put out the word, and people
hungry for work flocked to the gates. The company had the power
and made the selection. The employees had precious little power.

Today, of course, it's a whole different game. The balance of
power has shifted to talented people. The tipping point came a few
years ago when the economic expansion absorbed all the available
talent. For the first time since the Industrial Revolution, companies

69

were finding no one lining up at their gates. The initial response was to run some help-wanted ads, but that didn't bring a flood of résumés anymore.

What made it worse for companies was that this happened precisely when companies needed not just *more* people, but *more talented* people than ever before.

Companies jumped to pursue a host of aggressive hiring tactics: hiring bounties or tropical vacations for employees who suggested the most new hires, "flipping" company Web sites to get access to other companies' employee directories, and so on. But hiring gimmicks alone—regardless of how good they are—are not enough to win the war for talent. To *really* win on the recruiting front, you have to do much more. You must rebuild every part of your recruiting strategy. In this chapter, we show you how to do this by pumping talent in at all levels, by hunting for talent all the time, by tapping many diverse pools of talent, by finding passive job seekers, and more.

The frenzied pitch of the talent market in the late 1990s woke companies up to the need to rebuild their recruiting strategies and

Old Recruiting Strategies	New Recruiting Strategies
Grow all your own talent	Pump talent in at all levels
Recruit for vacant positions	Hunt for talent all the time
Go to a few traditional sources	Tap many diverse pools of talent
Advertise to job hunters	Find ways to reach passive candidates
Specify a compensation range and stay within it	Break the compensation rules to get the candidates you want
Recruiting is about screening	Recruiting is about selling as well as screening
Hire as needed with no overall plan	Develop a recruiting strategy for each type of talent

stimulated many creative new recruiting approaches. From time to time the economy will soften and recruiting may not seem like the crisis it once was. But wise companies will use any lulls in the talent wars to strengthen their talent pipeline and to opportunistically gain share in the talent market. Though you may want to reduce the quantity of people you hire during cooler periods, don't stop hiring high-quality talent—people who will be harder to win when the competition heats up again. The new recruiting strategies we recommend make good business sense in any economic environment and will be required to keep up with the competition for talent over the next couple of decades.

Pump Talent in at All Levels

For several generations, the corporate ladder was the dominant image for the way people moved through companies. People entered at the bottom, and if they were successful, climbed to the top. This was the contract between the company and the employee, one where the payoff came after fifteen or twenty years of service. Under this system, it was rare that an experienced manager was brought in from the outside and put in a position above a twenty-year veteran. Just ten years ago, it would have caused a heated stir, and certainly it would have appeared to the outside world as an admission that the company's development system had failed.

Yet in the last several years, that old paradigm has been shattered. It began to break in the early 1990s, when companies realized that they didn't have enough talented managers in their ranks to pursue all the opportunities and challenges they were facing. It crumbled further when they started losing large numbers of their managers to "new economy" start-ups and other companies. It was simply not possible to fill all those positions from within; companies began to raid competitors' talent to fill their vacancies. By the end of the decade, promoting exclusively from within, the cultural model that had existed since the beginning of the Industrial Revolution, was disappearing.

Hiring in at senior levels has advantages

For these reasons, some companies have begun to see the advantages of bringing talent in at more senior levels. Regularly bringing new people in is a good way to constantly calibrate—and even raise—the company's standards for talent. Of course, new people also bring fresh attitudes, new perspectives, and new ideas to the company.

Because they are committed to providing development and promotion opportunities for their own people, some companies have been reluctant to hire outsiders. It's easy to assume that hiring from the outside is inconsistent with development, but it isn't. Filling 10 percent to 25 percent of vacancies with outsiders will decrease the number of advancement opportunities for insiders a little bit, but not substantially. In fact, bringing first-rate leaders into midlevel and senior positions can provide admired role models for the more junior people.

GE, for instance, is regarded as one of the great developers of its own executive talent and continues to be primarily a "promote from within" company. Yet GE still brings in external hires at middle and senior levels. GE recognizes that external hiring, especially at the higher corporate levels, carries some risk, but the company is willing to assume that risk to expand its corporate gene pool. In fact, of the roughly 75 positions in the top 500 that become vacant each year, GE regularly fills about 20 percent from outside the organization.

Some executives worry that outside hires will destroy their company's culture. Bringing in a large number of outsiders all at once will probably change the culture, and in some cases this may be beneficial. But we believe that filling only 20 percent of non-CEO vacancies from the outside will not substantially change the corporate culture, and it could be just the breath of fresh air—and expertise—the company needs.

The Home Depot is an example of a company that has recently begun hiring from the outside—after years of strictly bringing its leaders up through the ranks. The Home Depot opened its doors in Atlanta in 1979. Ten years later, with about 145 stores nationwide, some of the first managers hired had climbed up to the top managerial ranks. This was consistent with the promise of founders Bernie Marcus and Arthur Blank: Join us, do well in the stores, and rise as far as your abilities will take you.

By 1996, however, Blank realized that there was only room for so many 100,000-square-foot orange boxes dotting the United States. He and his top team developed a growth strategy to launch five major new initiatives: international, convenience stores, home design centers, Internet/direct, and greater emphasis on professional contractors. In a major change of policy, Blank vowed to hire "the best person in the world" to lead each of these initiatives—even if that person had to come from the outside.

He recognized that outsiders might be viewed as interlopers, not having paid their dues by wearing The Home Depot's orange aprons in the aisles for years. However, Blank reasoned that the existing managers were needed to keep growing the traditional Home Depot business by 200 or so stores a year, and he believed that new skill sets were needed for the new businesses.

In 1997 and 1998, Blank searched the world for the top talent he needed. He hired the COO of Ikea, the Swedish furniture chain, to head International; the number three executive at Macy's to lead Diversified Businesses including Expo, the home design center; the COO of Orchard Supply, a successful California hardware convenience store chain to lead Convenience; a top manager from Disney to head up their Internet and direct business; and the CFO from one of GE's businesses to be their new CFO. He wasn't kidding when he said the best in the world.

Within two years, one of the five new executives had left the company, but the other four remained, and The Home Depot had forever changed its approach to hiring. In fact, in late 2000 the company hired GE executive Bob Nardelli, who had run GE's locomotive and turbine divisions, and was one of the two senior executives at GE who was not chosen to succeed CEO Jack Welch. Although

Nardelli had little consumer or retail experience, he is known as a hard negotiator with suppliers and a very hard worker himself, requisites for The Home Depot's culture. Blank vacated his position, first to become co-chair of the company with Bernie Marcus and subsequently to retire, so that Nardelli could have the CEO job. "Realizing that we had a terrific opportunity to add a business superstar to The Home Depot," Blank said, "we moved quickly."[2]

Similarly, as discussed in chapter 2, when SunTrust Banks decided in 1996 that it needed 600 new relationship managers to boost its growth, it decided to break with its traditional hire-from-within policy. The move was a shock to a culture that traditionally hired only at entry levels: They hired bright college graduates and grew them over three to seven years into midlevel managers. However, the bank had come to the conclusion that it couldn't meet its goals—which included double-digit growth—without adding more and even better managers to the mix.

Bill Rogers, then the Executive Vice President of Corporate Banking in the Atlanta bank, was one of the pioneers of this change. He began by trying to determine what kinds of people currently employed by the bank could serve as models for new hires. "I asked myself, 'Who are the best salespeople we have?'" To answer this question, he and his senior executive team quintiled their account executives based on their performance. Then, with the help of an industrial psychologist, the top-quintile people were assessed on their quantitative skills, selling characteristics, experience, and leadership style. "This profile," he explains, "became the bar by which we judged future hires. It gave us the confidence we needed."

Armed with this profile, Rogers and his team began to look outside the bank for the candidates they needed—relationship managers with five to ten years of experience. He encouraged his managers to come up with names of candidates. He also asked the bank's clients, "Who is the best competitor of ours that calls on you?" For very specific and specialized hiring needs, they engaged the help of search firms. When candidates were discovered, Rogers invited them in for interviews. Eventually an industrial psychologist administered standardized tests to assess each candidate's quantitative, verbal, and selling skills. They were similarly reviewed to determine how they would fit into SunTrust's culture. "We asked tough questions," Rogers recalls. "We concentrated on finding applicants whose work ethic, interpersonal skills, and values would indicate that they could assimilate easily and be successful." Over the next eighteen months, Rogers and his five key managers spent 50 percent of their time recruiting, screening, cultivating, and assimilating new people.

Their persistence paid off. Within two years, Rogers's division had doubled the size of its sales force from forty to eighty people. Because the new hires had much more experience than the average existing salespeople, the infusion raised the bar for the entire sales force. Before long, profitability for Rogers's corporate banking unit increased substantially, and the number of new clients doubled. Even the best of the existing account executives raised their sales productivity significantly. "Of the top people we hired into key positions," Rogers boasts, "almost 100 percent have stayed with us. More than half of our top-quintile account executives are now newcomers. In fact three of our top five relationship managers weren't here two years ago."

Managers across SunTrust's twenty four banks were having similar success. In the first year, SunTrust hired 600 new relationship managers, increasing the overall sales force by 20 percent. This allowed them to more than double their growth rate from 1996 through 1999.

Mitigating the risks of mid- and senior-level hiring

Hiring people from the outside does involve some risk. Failure rates of senior external hires can typically be around 30 percent.[3] However, that shouldn't stop you from employing this powerful talent-building lever. When you consider the benefits, having 70 percent of these new hires succeed is far better than not trying at all. Rather than forego hiring from the outside, we urge you to get better at it. Learn how to reduce the failure rate.

Easier said than done, you might be thinking, but there are steps you can take to increase the success rate of outside hires. First, screen for cultural fit to reduce the strength of the organization's anti-body rejection. Studies have shown that poor cultural fit is a major cause of turnover for new hires.[4] Cultural fit doesn't mean hires have to come from the same industry—after all, one of the benefits of out-side hiring is bringing in people with new perspectives. But it does mean their leadership style and values have to be compatible with the company's culture. Insist that cultural fit be explicitly assessed and discussed as part of the recruiting process. That said, assessing fit isn't easy to do, so you might consider engaging the services of an industrial psychologist to help with this, as Bill Rogers did.

Second, provide a thoughtful assimilation process for each new senior hire. This should include an orientation to the formal aspects of the company such as its operating plans, strategic plans, and organization charts, but it should also include insights on the infor-mal aspects, such as how decisions are made and how to gain sup-port for initiatives. Early agreement on performance expectations and time frames should also be part of the process. Finally—and this step is all too often overlooked—the new executive should get assistance building his or her internal network and understanding the cultural idiosyncrasies of the organization.[5]

The Limited has instituted a deliberate process to help its sen-ior hires get a good start. In 1997, CEO Les Wexner began an aggressive hiring campaign to bring in a number of superstars from inside and outside the retailing industry. These new hires included new leaders for half of The Limited's businesses. He also brought in senior people as function heads—marketing, HR, finance, and plan-ning. This was just the beginning of an aggressive hiring campaign.

At first, the new people went straight into their jobs—with little help in getting acclimated to the company. "It was like throwing people into the deep end of the pool with a fifty-pound block tied to their leg," concedes Len Schlesinger, COO and Executive Vice President of Organization, Leadership, and HR. Needless to say, a large number of them didn't assimilate and ended up leaving.

Shaken by these failed attempts, Wexner started to question the aggressive hiring program.

Instead of abandoning the hiring push, however, The Limited set out to make it work by starting an ambitious assimilation program. New senior hires now spend their first two months in the company's "On Boarding" program. During this time they meet with each of the company's thirty top leaders, listening to their thoughts on strategy, performance, and challenges; and they shadow their counterpart in another business unit. They are handed a stack of the company's most important speeches, presentations, and articles to read to gain a historical understanding of the company. They get a primer on retail math and a guide to company acronyms and buzzwords.

Later, they spend several days in the stores, the distribution center, and the design office, after which they are required to present a report on what they learned and what suggestions they might have for improving those areas. By the time the recruits start their jobs, they are connected with the company, their business unit, their function, and the community. The "On-Boarding" program at The Limited is a good example of outside hires being given the support they need to make the transition as smooth and successful as possible.

Entry-level hiring is good fuel for the system

Just as it is important to pump talent in at middle and senior levels, it is also important to pump in talent at entry levels. Bringing a strong pipeline of young talent into the company fuels the system for years to come. It also allows you to instill, early on, the culture, values, and skills of the organization. Most companies hire at the entry level, of course, but they don't do it as well as they should.

When Jeff Skilling joined Enron in 1980 to start Enron Capital and Trade, he immediately hired a large number of experienced investment bankers, traders, and executives from the outside. Skilling also decided to bring in a steady stream of the very best college and M.B.A. graduates he could find to stock the company with talent. To do this, Skilling started the Analyst and Associate Program, which offers entry-level hires a great opportunity. For their first two years, the recruits are rotated through Enron's business units so they can learn the essentials of risk management and trading. Following that training, the recruits move on to one of Enron's business units or go back to school to gain further education. The most impressive thing about Enron's Analyst and Associate Program is its scale. Every year this program brings in 500 recruits.

To be sure, not every company can handle 500 new entry-level recruits annually, but most companies could do more entry-level hiring of leadership talent than they currently are. If your company isn't bringing in a significant number of highly talented young people each year, it is giving up an important talent-building tool.

Hunt for Talent All the Time

In the past, companies recruited people to fill vacant positions. When a position became vacant, the hiring manager wrote up a requisition, specified the exact requirements the candidate would need for this particular job, and then went looking. "I happen to need a basketball player today. Did Michael Jordan happen to just quit his job?" is how Professor John Sullivan, head of the HR Management program at San Francisco University, describes the traditional approach to hiring. As he points out, the chances of landing a superstar using this approach are not very good.[6]

This position-centric approach worked fine in a loose talent market, but in a tight market for managerial talent, companies must adopt a new strategy. Companies need to hunt for talent continuously so as to capture people when *they* are ready to make a move.

Opportunistic hiring may seem a little strange, but we've found three ways to make it work. First, identify the kind of job a candidate would fit and court that person until one of those jobs becomes available. Second, hire them with a specific position in mind, even though the slot is not currently open. While they are waiting for that position they can be doing special projects and getting to know the organization.

Third, create or earmark certain jobs that are suitable for mid- to senior-level hires. Strategic planning, business development, audit staff, and assistant plant manager are examples of jobs that could be earmarked as entry points for experienced people. Keep people in these intake jobs only for a short while (six to eighteen months) so they are vacated for the next incoming hire.

PerkinElmer makes opportunistic hiring a regular part of its recruiting strategy. In fact, it has retained a headhunter to constantly look for experienced people who would make good general managers. In PerkinElmer's case, the point of entry for these incoming people is the business development function, where the new recruits work on special projects and learn the business for twelve to eighteen months while they wait for the right line position to become available. This program allows PerkinElmer to hire people with little knowledge of their industry. So far, it has hired four people a year through this program. The first four left the "bullpen" within sixteen months and have been extremely successful.

John Danner, a former nuclear submarine engineer, is an example. Danner had left the Navy and was in consulting when PerkinElmer found him and discovered that he wasn't completely happy. Courting Danner at a distance for a few months, PerkinElmer finally asked Danner to meet with CEO Greg Summe. A few days later, Summe made Danner an offer.

It wasn't an easy sell, though. Danner waffled for two months, until he was assured that his first position with the company would lead quickly to even better opportunities. "They sold me on the promise that I could create opportunities for myself as a business developer that would lead to a second job loaded with ownership," he explained. Indeed, fifteen months after signing on, Danner became general manager of an $80 million biotech business, which he helped acquire for the company.

Rich Walsh, PerkinElmer's head of HR, reports, "Those are ideal situations. We want to bring in high-potential people with the right intrinsics, teach them about our company, grow them in our culture as they grow our business, and eventually when they're ready we hope they'll run a business."

GE, fifty times bigger than PerkinElmer, is a leader in opportunistic hiring. It now brings more than 100 people a year from consulting firms, accounting firms, the military, and other fields into its business development, corporate audit, and other "transition" assignments. Generally speaking, these new hires spend six to eighteen months in their transitional roles, contributing to special initiatives, audits, and other functions while they get to know the business and the organization. If, after eighteen months, the person has not been hired by one of the divisions into a line position, they usually leave. This system, which began at the corporate level, was so successful that it was replicated in each division.

Companies like PerkinElmer and GE—firms that regularly hire experienced people into these kinds of transition jobs—develop a good track record in the eyes of candidates. Potential recruits are more willing to make this leap of faith when they can see that others who have taken the same path are now successful in great jobs within the company.

Do you opportunistically search for candidates? Do you scout for recruits whenever you interact with your suppliers and customers? Do you use conferences and trade association meetings as opportunities to scout for talent? Do you keep tabs on the careers of prospective candidates, noticing, for instance, when they may have missed a promotion? Finally, do you watch for favorable macro trends, such as corporate or military downsizings, mergers, and the dot-com implosions, that might offer up good candidates?

Sears, Roebuck and Co., for instance, hired an entire group of twenty-five software engineers who didn't want to leave Boise, Idaho, when their employer, U.S. Bank, merged with First Bank Systems. This group loved living in Boise, had families there, knew they worked well as a team, and wanted to be hired as a group. They held weekly meetings at a food court and systematically passed word of their intentions to personal contacts, including staff at a Chicago bank.

The bank couldn't figure out how to structure the deal. Then someone on the bank staff mentioned the proposal to a friend who worked at Sears. He knew that Sears was planning to locate a technology center outside Chicago and had acquired a site in Austin. In the end, Boise, with a ready-made staff, looked better than Austin, and Sears located its facility there instead. The original group later recruited another 125 people to join them.[7]

Tap Many Diverse Pools of Talent

In the past, companies generally looked for an experienced candidate for a specific job—a round peg for a round hole. They didn't have to go very far to find them, either. Companies could go each year to the same few schools, competitors, or companies in related industries to meet their hiring needs.

As the war for talent persists, though, it is unlikely that companies will find enough great talent in the same few places. Now companies have to look farther afield. They are being forced to hire people who don't have the traditional background. In many ways, they're better for it.

A decade ago, for instance, most of the big consulting firms looked strictly to the top five or six M.B.A. schools for their recruits. However, as these firms grew and that pool remained essentially static, they had to look elsewhere. Several of them widened their net to include the top ten to fifteen M.B.A. programs. Others began hiring college undergraduates, and created a new consulting position called an analyst expressly for this purpose. Many also started hiring lawyers, doctors, physicists, and experienced business managers. As a result, some of the consulting firms have reduced their reliance on M.B.A.'s to half of their total hiring and have found the non-M.B.A.'s to be very successful.

Other kinds of businesses can also tap into a much broader pool of talent. Arrow Electronics is a good example. The company had drawn its recruits from the same ten schools for years. But by the end of the 1990s, the hot economy was drawing some of the talent elsewhere. Arrow realized it had to change its strategy.

That's when Arrow decided to participate as one of the corporate sponsors of the National Collegiate Sales Competition, an intercollegiate sales competition held annually at Baylor University in Waco, Texas. Juniors and seniors who are studying professional sales and who come from more than twenty small colleges in the United States and Canada compete against each other in role-playing exercises. At the end, the contestants win prizes—and Arrow generally gets its pick of the top-placing competitors.

Arrow also searches other industries for salespeople. "If we need someone with five years of sales experience, does that necessarily have to be in electronics sales?" asks Les Gillen, Director of Strategic Staffing. "Why can't we pick someone with a financial sales background who has successfully moved mortgages?" Indeed, Arrow has done just that, and has found that a financial salesperson, with some specific industry training, can be a good fit.

The military is another source Arrow has tapped. In 2000, it hired fifteen military officers, taking advantage of their training, cross-cultural experiences, knowledge of logistics management, and technical knowledge. Arrow especially likes to hire former military officers who have troop leadership experience. "People like that are versed in 'what if' analyses and other competencies that match the skill sets our jobs demand," explains Gillen. "That's as valuable to us as someone who knows about electronics."

Arrow also discovered that by dropping the electrical engineering degree from its requirements, it has been able to hire other kinds of engineers—chemical, civil, or industrial—into field application roles. Many of these hires have been very successful because they have strong interpersonal skills and can relate well to customers.

Arrow currently fills 25 percent of its sales and distribution jobs with "nontraditional" hires and expects this percentage to increase. Like many other companies, Arrow has found that new types of hires not only fill empty positions but also bring a fresh perspective and a rich vein of creativity to the company. Likewise, companies increasingly recognize the need to build a more diverse talent pool. This doesn't just mean more women and more visible minorities (although this is important). It also means people with different experiences, different education, different ways of thinking, and different problem-solving styles. Diversity of this kind builds the strength of an organization.

Dee Hock, the founder and CEO emeritus of Visa, expressed his belief in the importance of hiring for intrinsics rather than for specific experience or knowledge. He said, "Hire and promote first on the basis of integrity; second, motivation; third, capacity; fourth, understanding; fifth, knowledge; and last and least, experience. Without integrity, motivation is dangerous; without motivation, capacity is impotent; without capacity, understanding is limited; without understanding, knowledge is meaningless; without knowledge, experience is blind. Experience is easy to provide and quickly put to good use by people with all the other qualities."[8]

Hiring people who don't have a traditional background does pose challenges. It requires a careful assessment of the intrinsic skills and characteristics necessary for success. You won't be looking for people who fit the culture but, rather, people who can adapt to the culture—or in certain instances, people you sense can stretch the culture in productive ways. People from very different backgrounds will require more development and investment at the beginning, but as Arrow will attest, the efforts can pay off handsomely.

Brainstorm all of the possible groups you could look to as new sources of talent, as figure 4-1 indicates.

Develop Creative New Channels

The recruiting game is changing for yet another reason: It's no longer sufficient to target your efforts to people looking for a job; you have to reach people who aren't looking. Half of the 6,500 managers we surveyed in 2000 said there is a 30 percent or greater chance that they will leave their company in the next two years.[9] Two-thirds of managers who switched companies in the last three years said that they left their last job not because they were looking for a new job, but because a better offer came their way.[10] In other words, many talented people today are passive job seekers.

Figure 4-1 Brainstorming Tool

To generate ideas for new kinds of pools to tap, brainstorm all the possible dimensions of difference from the traditional candidate profile

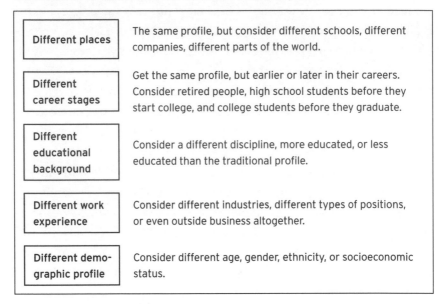

Different places	The same profile, but consider different schools, different companies, different parts of the world.
Different career stages	Get the same profile, but earlier or later in their careers. Consider retired people, high school students before they start college, and college students before they graduate.
Different educational background	Consider a different discipline, more educated, or less educated than the traditional profile.
Different work experience	Consider different industries, different types of positions, or even outside business altogether.
Different demo-graphic profile	Consider different age, gender, ethnicity, or socioeconomic status.

So there are lots of great people out there, but you have to lure them away from your competitors. For this reason, and because of the need to reach many different pools of talent, companies need new channels for reaching candidates.

The newest channel is, of course, the Internet. There are many ways a company can use the Internet to find candidates. You can attract prospective candidates when they visit the company's Web site, whether those people were looking for a job or not. You can post career opportunities on job boards and career sites, and you can search the résumés posted on job boards and by visitors to career sites.

The extremely hot market for IT talent in the late 1990s spurred many companies to develop creative Web-based recruiting techniques. Cisco was one of the leaders. Like a candy store for technophiles, the company's Web site is designed to lure potential employees in. Among the treats it offers are the Make Friends @ Cisco program, which connects site visitors with a Cisco employee who does work that interests the visitor; the Cisco Profiler, a witty interface that enables site surfers to create a résumé to send to the company; and an "Oh-No-My-Boss-Is-Coming" button that transmits a graphic of "Seven Habits of a Successful Employee" (about 90 percent of the site's hits come during business hours from those who work for others). In 1999, Cisco received more than 80 percent of prospective employees' résumés electronically and two-thirds of hires were recruited via the Internet.[11]

Using the Internet to manage the recruiting process can also help speed it up, which helps to fill jobs sooner and land candidates before they are lured elsewhere. Web-based recruiting applications can automate receiving résumés, initial screening tests, background checks, interview scheduling, communication with the candidate, sharing résumés across departments, and reporting.

Cisco's skillful Web-based recruiting process pruned many days off the time it takes to fill a job. Cisco reduced its recruiting cycle—the time from initial contact to the close of the deal—by 60 percent in three years, down from 113 days in 1996 to 45 days in 1999. That's precious time for the company and for the candidate.[12]

Databases are another new channel. Just as marketers reach out to customers, companies can build a relationship with prospective employees. Database recruiting is more like hunting with a harpoon than drift netting. It starts with identifying individuals who have the characteristics that you are looking for and who might want to work for the company one day. Stay in touch with those people over time, and let them know that you would like them to consider joining your company. Learn about the personal and career factors that might affect their career decisions, and try to convince them to join when the time might be right for them.

To build a database of prospects, think of all the people your organization has collectively known at one time or another: friends and colleagues of your current employees, candidates who turned down an offer, people not suitable for one part of the business who may be great for another, and strong performers who left your company. These résumés are out there somewhere, waiting to be mined.

In addition, actively search for people to add to your database: top performers at your competitors; people who speak at conferences or win awards; or people who are alumni of your target schools, associations, or companies.

Keep in touch with these people: Send them articles, invite them to events, and give them access to a Web site that has information of particular interest to them. Reach out to them from time to time and let them know they are always welcome to interview with your company.

Electronic Arts (EA), the world's largest video game company, uses its résumé database to keep in touch with game developers who might someday be recruited to the company. EA relies on its Web site to nurture the relationship: The first time a job seeker clicks "Jobs" at EA.com, he or she is asked questions about career goals and aspirations, backgrounds, interests, and capabilities. The Web script even asks permission to contact the candidate in the future. The system then notifies EA's hiring managers of possible matches and slots for each candidate. In less than a year, EA has assembled a pool of 34,000 potential candidates, 20,000 of whom have agreed to receive additional information.

Recently the system was put to the test. EA decided to move the development of its NASCAR game from Redwood City, California, to Orlando, Florida. The move required the quick hiring of forty local game developers. The solution was an interactive e-mail titled "Get in the Game" that invited 18,000 of the database's prequalified, previously assessed candidates to explore the new opportunities in Orlando. The details of the positions, required qualifications, and links to apply online were accompanied by a showcase of the studio's best graphics and animations, not to mention a sneak peek at a highly anticipated video game that was also developed in Orlando. Within days, 3,000 candidates clicked through to the Florida link for more information. From there, finding the necessary hires was easy.[13]

The Internet may be the newest recruiting channel, but the most effective means of finding recruits is still probably the oldest: personal referrals. Some 40 percent of the managers we surveyed in our original research were hired as a result of personal contacts.[15]

TALENT AGENTS FOR EXECUTIVES

For a long time, the only intermediaries in the recruiting process were executive search professionals, who represented the company's interests and helped find candidates. In today's market, where individuals have much more power, another type of intermediary is entering the talent market to represent individuals. Executives may soon have talent agents—just like movie stars—to help them find and negotiate the best jobs. Sound far-fetched?

There already are executive talent agents in operation today. One talent agent has about thirty clients. He counsels them, represents them, does PR for them, and markets them.[14] Another executive agent builds deals around his CEO clients. He searches for the right business opportunity and the right financial backers. He coaches his clients to never say the "J-word." It isn't a *job* he's getting for them—it's a business deal.

We predict this is just the beginning of what will become a widespread phenomenon, starting with senior executives and spreading to lower tier executives. Think of the advantages for the individual: someone to constantly scout for the next best opportunity, to handle all those calls from headhunters, and to provide advice during compensation negotiations.

Think about how this will change the dynamic between companies and individuals. Think about how this will change the recruiting process.

Recruits referred by employees also tend to be quite successful. Surprisingly, though, few companies are deliberate and organized about mining the vast network of relationships that their current employees have to offer.

Everyone in the company should be a talent scout. Through participation in the right associations, conferences, online mailing lists, chat rooms, and visits to customers and suppliers, they should build their own network of candidates. Tap the resource that lies dormant in the contact lists of all the company's employees.

DoubleClick has generated hundreds of candidate leads by tapping into the personal networks of its employees. It used an employee referral program to hire 500 people in the first three months of 2000, growing the company by 30 percent. Rewarding people who delivered referrals helped: In addition to two Harley Davidsons rewarded to those who submitted the most referrals, employees got $1,000 for their first referral, $2,000 for their second, and so on, without a ceiling. Altogether, the employee referral program accounted for 43 percent of DoubleClick's new hires.

Be creative about the many different ways you might be able to reach candidates. There are endless possibilities for how you might open a dialogue between a potential hire and the company.

One company held a two-day, nearly round-the-clock telethon in which eighty employees, including company brass, called qualified candidates. One had a video game on its Web site and invited the high scorers to apply for programming jobs. Another invited hackers to break into its system and invited those with the most creative approaches to a job in its IT group.[16]

Break the Compensation Rules to Get Who You Want

In today's talent market, where top candidates are in high demand and the value they create is tremendous, companies need to pay what it takes to get great candidates. After the extended effort of finding, selecting, and wooing a great candidate, don't let that person slip away because he or she is expecting more money than you had in mind. In other words, if you *think* you're paying enough to get good people, but you're not getting them, think again.

SunTrust's Bill Rogers learned this when he tried to recruit forty relationship managers with SunTrust's existing compensation structure (which consisted of a below-average salary augmented by big bonuses). It was an average compensation package, Rogers soon learned, and it wasn't attracting the A-level talent he had targeted.

So Rogers stepped up to the plate and started offering signing bonuses, paying moving expenses, and guaranteeing first-year bonuses. Eventually, he also bumped salaries up beyond the industry average—a first for SunTrust. It was an expensive move, but it worked. "Almost all of the new relationship managers have more than paid back what we originally invested to hire them," Rogers

Figure 4-2 Pay What It Takes to Hire the Right People

% of corporate officers who strongly agree

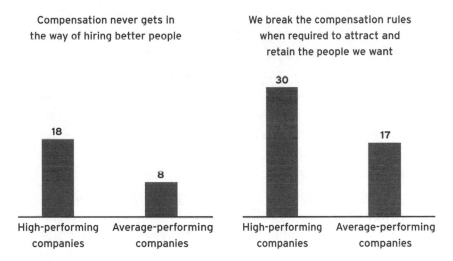

Compensation never gets in
the way of hiring better people

We break the compensation rules
when required to attract and
retain the people we want

Source: McKinsey & Company's War for Talent 2000 Survey

explains. "We would have gotten few of them if we had been unwilling to up the ante on compensation."

To win in this new market, you can't play compensation by the old rules. You have to ask yourself two important questions: How much will it take to get them? and How much value will this person create for my business?

The answer may be outside the compensation range you originally planned to pay. You may have to increase the top end of the range, or creatively use signing bonuses and other perks to raise compensation without disrupting the salary structure. The higher-performing companies are more willing to pay what it takes to hire the people they need (see figure 4-2).

Execute a Flawless Selling Process

In the past, the recruiting process was focused mostly on *screening*. Companies carefully chose the best people from a long line of good candidates. They could afford to take their time while the candidates waited nervously for a decision.

In today's talent market, it's the company's job to *sell* itself to the candidate. Yes, companies still have to be rigorous in the selection decision, but the harder part is convincing people to join the company, or to even listen to an offer. Every step of the process has to be a flawlessly executed courtship: persuasive, delightful, and artful. The candidate should feel sought after and valued. Every interaction should leave him or her thinking, "Would I love to be a part of that organization!"

In the past, companies didn't send their best people out on talent hunts; they sent people they could spare. This isn't the way to hook great talent today.

You need to have your high performers on the front lines of recruiting. Line managers should spend a day or two each month recruiting—interviewing candidates, making presentations on campuses, and persuading candidates to accept offers. Your highest performers should lead the recruiting strategy. HR managers should be orchestrating the process, not standing between the hiring managers and the candidates.

To get the best candidates, companies must play their best cards. "Recruiting the best talent was my sole goal the first year I was here," says Steve Macadam, Vice President of Georgia-Pacific's Packaging Division. "I worked closely with our human resources team to iron out the logistics involved with recruiting. But when it came to the hard sell and closing the deal, you better believe it was priority number one on my list. I personally flew around the country visiting prospects and spending as much time with them as they needed."

Macadam knew the only way to get people to believe in his leadership and join his team was to be there himself. He advises, "Any manager who wants to get the best people working for him had better go get them himself." Of the ninety-six people hired during Macadam's first eighteen months, forty-nine were personally interviewed and courted by him. Twenty-nine of those forty-nine are considered to have high potential for future leadership and almost all are still with the company.

John Thompson, Symantec's CEO, also understands the power of the personal touch. Symantec is a security software company based in Cupertino, California, best known for its Norton Utilities and Norton AntiVirus product lines. Thompson recalls a situation when the director of his research lab, a superstar, was lured to a dot-com. "I wrote him an e-mail note that said, 'I'm surprised. I thought you loved our company. And I thought you understood how important you were to what we're trying to get done. But I guess you didn't. Shame on us. I wish you the best,'" Thompson recalls. A week later the research director was back. He sent a note back to Thompson: "I'm back, and I do love this company."

There's another good reason to put your best people on recruiting: The people doing the recruiting are setting the standard for talent for the company. The caliber of talent they have in their minds is going to determine how high your organization will fly. As Sir Arthur Conan Doyle said, "Mediocrity knows nothing higher than itself, but talent instantly recognizes genius."

Develop a Recruiting Strategy for Each Division

We all know what a marketing strategy is like. Each customer segment is identified and sized, and its unique needs are profiled. A value proposition and pricing strategy for each segment is developed. Channels, tactics, and sales force programs are prepared. Target market share and sales goals are agreed on. Highly skilled marketing and sales managers spend hundreds of hours preparing these robust, written plans. The executive committee discusses and agrees on these marketing plans.

But does your company have a written *recruiting* strategy? For each division? For each type of talent? Is it as robust as your marketing strategy? Probably not. Before the war for talent, who needed such a rigorous exercise? But now a recruiting strategy that

Figure 4-3 Recruiting Strategy for Division ABC for Year 2001

Type of Talent	Hiring Goal	Sources and Channels	Our Value Proposition Message	Responsibility	Measures of Success
Software programmers	100	15 universities	"State-of-art technology"	3 unit heads 5 school managers	Acceptance rate; cost per hire
Experienced electrical engineers	50	Employee referrals and Internet	"Choose your job and location"	2 mfg managers 1 HR manager	Number hired; performance in first year
General managers	20	6 M.B.A. schools, 2 search firms looking for consultants	"A line job in 18 months"	Corporate heads of planning and finance	Percentage in top 20 percent of class

Attached page for each talent type:

· Number of hires from each source/channel

· Profile of target candidate

· Interview and screening process

· Compensation range and options

looks across the business, one as detailed as the marketing strategy, is required.

Here's what we recommend: Ask each division to develop a recruiting strategy. In the first year, it can be as simple as the one illustrated in figure 4-3. The second year, look for opportunities across functions or types of talent to share best practices and candidates across divisions.

Reflect with your leadership team and HR department on how you can shape your recruiting strategy to pump talent in at all levels, continuously hunt for talent, tap many diverse talent pools, develop creative new channels, break the compensation rules when necessary, and execute a flawless selling process.

Hiring great people is going to be increasingly important to your company's performance, and the competition in the talent market is going to get increasingly sophisticated at luring talent. Make sure your organization has a robust recruiting strategy that will help you win more than your fair share of talent.

5

WEAVE
DEVELOPMENT INTO
YOUR ORGANIZATION

In George Bernard Shaw's *Pygmalion*, Eliza Doolittle, the ragged Cockney girl, comes to the attention of a famed phonetics expert, Professor Henry Higgins. Higgins takes Doolittle under his wing to prove that his personal attention can transform Eliza into a lady with a perfect command of the King's English. Higgins eventually succeeds beyond his own dreams, transforming Eliza and himself in the process. It makes for a great play, a classic motion picture and, as we all know, a great musical, *My Fair Lady*.

But it also formed the core observation of a classic *Harvard Business Review* article, "Pygmalion in Management," first published in 1969—and reprinted almost continuously ever since. In the article, author J. Sterling Livingston explained the vital role that managers play in developing their subordinates: "Although most top executives have not yet diagnosed the problem, industry's greatest challenge by far is to rectify the under-development, under-utilization and ineffective management and use of its most valuable resource—its young managerial and professional talent."[1]

The challenge remains. As Professor Higgins discovered, and as Livingston reiterated, talent rarely arrives fully developed. People possess vast amounts of potential that, when nurtured and challenged, can be brought into full bloom.

Take Emily Hickey, for example. Hickey is no Eliza Doolittle. She attended the University of North Carolina at Chapel Hill, and graduated cum laude with a double degree in English and religious studies. She never had to sell flowers in the open market for a living. Like Eliza, though, Emily wasn't prepared for the wider world. It took a mentor to open doors for her, encourage her, and challenge her to realize her potential.

Following graduation, Emily landed an entry-level job with a technology consulting firm. She did well, and that was reflected in her six-month review, but something was missing. She felt she could do more, but nobody saw that. Nobody gave her the opportunity to extend the boundaries of her potential. Emily realized she would not find personal challenges and development opportunities at her current job.

After looking around, Emily accepted an offer at a company that was in its developmental stages. The company published an Internet job board, which later became known as HotJobs.com. At HotJobs she found the stretch opportunities she was looking for. She started out as an account manager, then worked with company engineers on SoftShoe, the software that runs the HotJobs.com site. She eventually became the company spokesperson for SoftShoe and accepted a prestigious prize for the software at the Comdex computer show. Next, she was named Vice President of Product Management, where she built the team, processes, and product strategies from scratch. Once Product Management was humming, she helped turn around a software company HotJobs acquired and managed the P&L for one of its products.

Thanks to her own talent and hard work, Emily succeeded. But there was another element at play: Without the personal mentoring and encouragement she received from former CEO Richard Johnson, she admits she wouldn't have gotten so far so fast. "When I first met Richard, I immediately recognized him as someone with the opposite set of talents as I possessed," Emily says. "I could see that he knew how to speak and debate persuasively, how to position ideas aggressively, how to act with self-confidence. I wanted to emulate him, to learn from him."

But learning from Johnson wasn't easy, she admits. Her boss was demanding. One time, he pushed her in front of a group of journalists to give a major software presentation. She won "best in show" for that presentation, but that was just the beginning. "Since then he has consistently been pushing me into presentations at board meetings, investor conferences, and business development meetings," she says. "It means a lot to me that he puts me in high-impact situations, lets me screw up, criticizes me, then turns around and puts me right back up there." She adds, "He doesn't let me dwell on my screw-ups. I totally blew one presentation and he immediately told me I wasn't ready for prime time. But a few weeks later he slated me to present something to the board, which I nailed. It made me more confident, in a way, because he had totally schooled me."

For Emily, Johnson's willingness to stretch her and to provide feedback and coaching has made a big difference. "I've been exposed to situations where I've been expected to act like a manager with twenty years' experience," she says. "I feel as if I've had a career compacted into two years."

To win the war for talent, companies must develop their people. Not everyone can be developed into a superstar. But everybody can push the limits of what they can accomplish when given a real challenge, a dose of encouragement, and the support they need to succeed. Those companies that weave development into the fabric of their organization will attract more talent, hold onto it longer, and perform better in the long run.

It seems like an easy message to grasp. But consider this:

- Fifty-four percent of corporate officers said their inability to develop their people into great executives was a huge or major obstacle to strengthening their talent pool.[2]

- Fifty-seven percent of managers believe that their company *does not* develop people quickly and effectively.[3]

- Managers who feel their company develops them poorly are five times more likely to leave than people who feel their company develops them well.[4]

- Fifty-seven percent of managers who intend to leave their current employer in the next two years cited insufficient development and learning opportunities as a critical or very important reason for leaving; 69 percent cited insufficient career advancement opportunities.[5]

How can you transform more of your Eliza Doolittles into leaders who are confident and whose greatest potential as human beings is realized? How can you make your Henry Higginses into more thoughtful and inspiring leaders? That's what we will explore in the rest of this chapter.

Development is poorly delivered in most companies. To win the war for talent, companies must improve their ability to cultivate the potential of their people. They must start using job experiences to help drive development, they must give their people constant coaching and feedback, and they must make mentoring a reality throughout their organizations.

Old Approach to Development	New Approach to Development
Development just happens	Development is woven into the fabric of the organization
Development means training	Development primarily means challenging experiences, coaching, feedback, and mentoring
The unit owns the talent; people don't move across units	The company owns the talent; people move easily around the company
Only poor performers have development needs	Everyone has development needs and receives coaching
A few lucky people find mentors	Mentors are assigned to *every* high-potential person

How People Grow

Many leaders don't understand how managers grow. They think training is the key to development. But when we asked managers in our survey what fueled their development throughout their careers, it was not training; it was job experiences. That came as no surprise to us. What was surprising was the high degree of importance they assigned to coaching, feedback, and mentoring (see figure 5-1).

The Dearth of Development

Another surprise was how poorly development is delivered at most companies. When we asked managers how well their current company delivers on the various components of development, only 39 percent of the managers said that their company is very effective at providing candid feedback, only 37 percent said that their company is very effective at providing mentoring, and only 47 percent said that their company is very effective at advancing high performers quickly.[6]

Why are companies doing such a poor job with development? We believe it is because they don't recognize the link between great development and business performance. Perhaps, too, it is because most managers themselves have never benefited from great development. Therefore, they are ill equipped to drive it in their own organizations. Additionally, it is not expected, valued, or measured in most companies.

Many managers feel uneasy with the emotional and personal involvement great talent development requires. Being a good coach or mentor requires knowing and discussing your people's talents and potential in ways that may seem almost intrusive. Some managers are uncomfortable doing this. We hope that those who fall into this category will push themselves beyond their comfort zone (as we saw Mimi Breeden do in chapter 3) to engage in what can be a remarkably rewarding experience: helping another person develop his or her most extraordinary self.

Figure 5-1 Factors That Drive Development

% of middle and senior managers

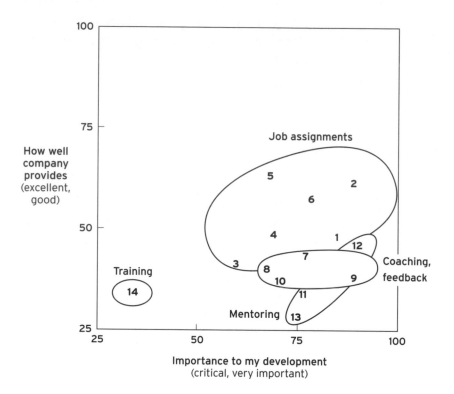

JOB ASSIGNMENTS
1 Promote high performers quickly
2 Build skills to boost career prospects
3 Fast rotation and advancement
4 Roles with P & L responsibility
5 Special project opportunities
6 On-the-job training

COACHING, FEEDBACK
7 Told my strengths and weaknesses
8 360° feedback

9 Candid, insightful feedback
10 Informal coaching from boss

MENTORING
11 Great mentor
12 Great senior role models
13 Mentoring advice on development

TRAINING
14 Traditional classroom training

Source: McKinsey & Company's War for Talent 2000 Survey

Use Job Experiences to Drive Development

Academics and researchers have been talking for years about the primary role job experience plays in developing people.[7] Yet many companies underattend to the critical decisions they make every day on how they deploy people.

Keep the learning curve steep

"If managers are unskilled, they leave scars on the careers of young people, cut deeply into their self-esteem, and distort their image of themselves as human beings," wrote J. Sterling Livingston. "But if we are skillful and have *high expectations*, subordinates' self-confidence will grow, their capabilities will develop and their productivity will be high."[8] As noted by Livingston, people need new challenges and experiences to grow. They need to be given assignments that they don't yet know how to do. This is particularly true for your high-potential people.

General Electric is very deliberate about giving people stretch assignments, viewing it, in fact, as placing strategic bets on its talented people. Chuck Okosky, former Vice President of Executive Development, notes, "Bet on the natural athletes, the ones with the strongest intrinsic skills, people who have demonstrated the ability to assemble and excite a high-quality team, and the intensity to do a tough job well. Don't be afraid to promote stars without specifically relevant experience, seemingly over their heads. Generally you will be surprised at how well they do."

The Home Depot also keeps the learning curve steep for high performers. The average age at which managers get their first P & L job is twenty-six. One store manager told us that he started at the company at eighteen, became a department manager at twenty-one, an assistant store manager at twenty-three, and then a store manager at twenty-five! Not everyone at The Home Depot enjoys such a quick ascent, but the company's philosophy is to take chances on those who seem ready to make the leap.

Timing is important, too. Moving people too fast can erode accountability for results and can shortchange learning. Moving them too slowly holds back the pace of development. Most companies err on the side of moving too slowly. When reviewing your high-potential people, ask yourself, "Has their learning curve flattened out? Could they take on a bigger challenge?"

Give people different kinds of challenges

People need not only bigger jobs, they need different kinds of jobs. In *The Lessons of Experience*, Lombardo, McCall, and Morrison identified the different kinds of challenges that are important development experiences. These include line-to-staff switches, starting projects from scratch, and fixing businesses in trouble, among others.[9] Well-rounded general managers should experience many of these different types of challenges during their careers.

Amgen is a company that deliberately gives high-potential people exposure to a variety of jobs. For instance, Amgen Vice President Keith Leonard started in logistics, moved to finance, took an international assignment in the Netherlands, then a posting in sales and marketing, and was finally tapped to head a new rheumatology unit. Executive Vice President Dennis Fenton, who was trained as a molecular biologist, has a similar story. He used to lead sales and marketing, and is now responsible for operations at Amgen, which includes manufacturing, logistics, engineering, quality, information management, and, most recently, research. "I'm certainly feeling stretched at this point," he admits, "but that's the essence of life— pushing yourself to your limits to see what you can do."

Amgen doesn't throw its people into the deep end without life preservers, of course. It provides mentoring, coaching, and continual review for people who are put into stretch jobs in order to help them swim rather than sink.

Give people high-octane special project assignments

Special project assignments—those with specific objectives lasting a few months—are particularly good development opportunities.

They usually require targeted problem solving, a cross-functional integrated approach, teamwork, exposure to senior executives, and the need to persuade rather than direct. People can often participate in these assignments part time while still holding their regular job. As mentioned in chapter 3, Arrow Electronics provides special assignments by putting people temporarily into positions that are open while the incumbent takes a sabbatical.

Continuously stretch the boundaries of their current job

Even while in the same job, people can be stretched and challenged. Rather than thinking about a job as rigidly and explicitly defined, think of it as having a broad charter. Challenge people to reconceptualize their roles, to reorient their responsibilities, and to do the job as it has never been done before.

Encourage people to identify opportunities to relaunch a product, market it to a new country, improve a customer relationship, or mentor a high-potential individual. Give them stretch opportunities, from the handling of a difficult negotiation to the presentation of an important report to the board. Remember, the job doesn't define the individual's potential in the role; the individual defines the potential he or she will contribute and the direction in which he or she will take the job. Try to imagine what a job could be with different leadership, or find the person who can take the old job off its current trajectory and raise it to a steeper one.

Structure jobs so they are more developmental

When designing the organization, consider flattening its structure and decentralizing the work. Jobs with P & L responsibility, for instance, provide more opportunity to grow general management capabilities, and cross-functional teams give people the chance to broaden their perspective. Johnson & Johnson, for instance, has more than 190 operating companies.[10] That amount of decentralization helps the company foster an entrepreneurial climate in which young people get early responsibility and skill-stretching opportunities.

Pay special attention to some jobs

Some jobs are particularly useful in developing future company leaders. The five jobs that managers in our survey rated as most important to their development were: a position with larger scope; turning around a business; starting a new business; a large, high-profile special project; and working outside their home country.[11] These jobs are in limited supply in most organizations, so they should be carefully assigned to the highest potential talent.

At Amgen, for example, product development team leaders are considered to be key development positions, as they require the leader to take the product all the way from research and clinical development through to marketing and regulatory issues. Because this position is so cross-functional and all-embracing, Amgen CEO Kevin Sharer considers it an important path for senior executives. Sharer believes that if a manager cannot successfully lead a product development team, he or she won't likely be able to lead the company someday.

GE viewed the key Six Signs positions as important development opportunities during the kick-off of its quality program. It set out to staff these "Black Belt" positions with its highest potential people. Following this experience, these high-potential leaders were put into bigger operating roles in the company. It didn't take long for them to transfer their stretch experiences into higher performance throughout GE. But the Black Belt positions were more than just good development opportunities; they were critical to driving GE's performance.

Like GE and Amgen, companies should ensure that the highest-potential people are deployed against the most developmental jobs, *and* the most critical jobs are staffed with the most talented people.

Design the deployment process to promote development

Most companies match people with positions in a way that doesn't optimize development: The hiring manager looks at the people he or she knows and picks the "most qualified" person for the job. Because managers are typically unaware of all the potential talent throughout the company, they tend to pick someone nearby. They miss the opportunity to grow the highest-potential people and they are disinclined to take risks on people. Amgen is trying to avoid this mistake. "Usually you would fill a job with a person whose CV looks tailor made," explains Ilana Meskin, Senior Director of Human Resources at Amgen. "Now we're filling that position with a real talent lens. Who's going to get the most stretch? Who's going to learn the most and how are we going to use that vacancy to expressly develop someone?"

The deployment process should access talent from anywhere in the organization and should explicitly factor in development. This starts with the philosophy that the top 200 to 500 managers are not operating unit or staff unit assets, but corporate assets. Only when companies view people as corporate assets will talent flow freely to the most attractive opportunities.

To institute this philosophy, the CEO needs to start questioning the practice of promoting the next obvious person in line. With the support of the head of executive development, the CEO should become involved in staffing the top 200 to 500 managerial positions. The final decisions on hiring should normally lie with the hiring manager, but the CEO should ensure that a broad slate of candidates from throughout the company is considered. The CEO should play a particularly strong role in those positions that are especially important in developing future leaders and driving the company's performance.

Two approaches to deployment

There are two approaches that can be used to ensure an effective deployment process. The first is the chessboard approach, in which the CEO and head of executive development plan a chessboard of moves that will optimize deployment across the company. For each vacancy, they develop a slate of candidates, which they discuss with the hiring manager. Then the hiring manager makes the final decision. Individuals' preferences are taken into consideration, but the individuals are not the ones actively putting their names on the slate.

The second strategy is the open market approach, in which the individuals and the hiring managers generally find each other. Individuals seek out the opportunities they are interested in and submit their names for consideration. The hiring manager hunts for good candidates, considers all the candidates who have presented themselves as interested in the position, and then makes the hiring decision. The CEO reviews the decisions, and may choose to get involved in some of them, but usually lets the market work it out.

GE uses the chessboard approach for its top 500 management positions.[12] Jack Welch, with the help of Bill Conaty, the Head of HR, and Chuck Okosky, until recently the Head of Executive Development, were actively involved in all assignment decisions for these 500 jobs. GE's management makes it clear that the corporate center orchestrates the staffing of these positions.

When a position needed to be filled, Welch, Conaty, and Okosky would typically prepare a slate of candidates. The slate relied heavily on the information and insights developed in Session C, GE's annual talent review process. It included obvious candidates as well as counterintuitive candidates who were added to the mix to challenge the conventional wisdom about the right person for the job. The trio also considered recent performance assessments and each candidate's own view of career options and preferences as articulated through the talent review process. In the end, the hiring manager selected the person for the job.

The advantage of the chessboard approach is its ability to optimize across a set of moves. It allows the organization to make sure that the most capable people are being deployed against the most important opportunities.

On the other hand, many companies, including Enron, SAS Institute, Hewlett-Packard, and many consulting firms, use the open market approach. At Hewlett-Packard, for example, there is a strong tradition of high-potential people moving across business units, geographies, and functions. Individuals are expected to "pack their own chute" as they manage their career paths, and managers comb the organization to identify high-potential people they can bring into their unit. There is a firm "no hoarding" policy that makes it very clear that managers are not to stand in the way of their people moving to other areas.

There are three formal processes at Hewlett-Packard that provide the backbone of this largely informal system. First, all individuals are given a performance rating based on forced distribution (so managers can simplify their search by scouting around for the 4s and 5s). Second, all managers have access to a résumé book of high-potential people selected for the advanced training program. Third, there is a job-posting system for all jobs except the top 100, making it easy for individuals to find attractive opportunities.

The open market approach has a number of benefits. By being actively involved in finding their own jobs, people are more likely to feel engaged and challenged. Additionally, the open market system forces managers to keep their businesses vibrant and alluring, for without these qualities they won't be able to attract the talent they need.

As HP illustrates, three elements need to be in place in order for the open market approach to achieve the optimal match of people and jobs across the entire company: a rigorous assessment process so that hiring managers have a credible source of information about individuals' performance and potential; a job-posting system so that people can readily see all available opportunities; and a "no hoarding" policy so managers don't block their best people from moving to new opportunities.

Provide Constant Coaching and Feedback

In addition to challenging assignments, people must be given feedback and coaching about their strengths and weaknesses. People need to be told how well they are performing, what specific things they are excelling at, and what they should do to improve their performance. Not telling people these things robs them of the opportunity to take charge of their development and their careers. As Morgan McCall points out in *High Flyers: Developing the Next Generation of Leaders*, lack of feedback often plays a role in the derailment of highly talented people.[13] Self-awareness is critical to their continued growth.

Yet only 35 percent of individuals feel their company tells them openly and candidly where they stand.[14] How well do you give the people you work with candid, helpful feedback and coaching?

Feedback tells people what they excel at and what they should improve. Coaching provides instruction, guidance, and support for making those changes happen. Ideally, it also includes storytelling, even about the boss's own personal experiences. Stories instruct, comfort, and show the human side of the boss. People need both. Feedback should be balanced; otherwise it can be demoralizing. It should be coupled with coaching; otherwise it's unhelpful.

Every manager should be a coach, but most aren't. As McCall noted, "Personal change is an emotional undertaking. Uncertainty, fear, loss, damage to self-esteem, intimidation, and humiliation are significant and potentially debilitating emotions. . . . As with any weighty challenge, knowing that people care about you and will offer support, can help someone hold on, try again, get back up, and otherwise persevere."[15]

When Larry Bossidy became CEO of AlliedSignal, he dramatically increased performance expectations for each of his top people. He also realized that success would require a quantum leap in candor and coaching. About eight months after arriving on the job, Bossidy began writing a two-page feedback memo annually to each of his ten direct reports. The letters were simple, focusing on strengths and areas for development. He also spent about an hour with each manager, rigorously comparing the individual's performance to the expectations Bossidy had set at the previous session. He encouraged each of his direct reports to exercise similar openness with their direct reports, making it "OK to have and work on development needs."

Then Bossidy did something particularly unusual. He shared the feedback on his people with the board of directors. He did this for two reasons: to prove to the board that he, too, would be held accountable for the quality of the talent pool he developed, and to prove to his subordinates that the reviews he shared with them were "the full story and nothing but the story." He couldn't overemphasize his belief in candid, honest, helpful feedback.

Bossidy also believes that most CEOs are unaware of the lack of feedback their subordinates are receiving. "If you ask any CEO if their direct reports know what the CEO thinks of them," said Bossidy, "the CEO will slam the table and say, 'Absolutely! I'm with them all the time. I travel with them. We are always discussing their results.'" But, he added, "If you then ask the direct reports the same question, nine out of ten will say, 'I don't have a clue, I haven't had a performance review or any feedback in the last five years.'" Indeed we were amazed to hear manager after manager, even in some well-managed companies, say they had not had a candid, helpful, written performance review in years.

The unnatural act

Why isn't there more coaching and candid feedback? For most of us, giving candid feedback is uncomfortable. It's hard to do. It takes precious time. Many people don't know how to do it well because they never experienced it themselves. Organizations don't explicitly value it or hold people accountable for delivering it.

Part of the problem may be in the word *candor*. Candor is not mean-spirited criticism, nor is it exclusively negative feedback. Candor is an open, respectful dialogue about an individual's achievements, coupled with an insightful acknowledgment of challenges, or even failures, that stand between the individual and the next success. It's an appropriate mix of constructive criticism and positive feedback. Underpinning it should be genuine caring for the individual's growth and development.

Most managers gloss over or omit the constructive criticism. They know it can be the start of a sometimes uncomfortable dialogue. When delivered with a genuine dose of caring, though, it can be received more openly. You can't go soft on coaching and feedback, but you can deliver it more empathetically.

The truth can hurt, but it doesn't have to

As you think about delivering feedback to others, try to imagine the tables turned. The truth hurts. You've felt it. Remember your last candid feedback session?

It happens once a year (if you're lucky) and lasts 30 minutes. Your boss has the sheet of paper with The Verdict. He starts by congratulating on your accomplishments, but it feels glib and you're already tuning him out. You have that gnawing feeling in your stomach as you prepare for the other shoe to drop. You've hardly absorbed a word of praise because you're anticipating those transitional words (*however/but/on the other hand*) that will signal he's about to discuss your "opportunities for growth" or whatever other euphemism is being used for your weaknesses.

He shifts in his chair, tacitly expressing his own unease with the next part of the conversation, and outlines three gaps in your performance you need to address. You're feeling a whirlwind of emotions: hurt, defensive, worried there's some truth to what you just heard, and misunderstood. Then there's the pause. It's your turn. You search for the poise to respond to the feedback. You take a deep breath.

This is not far from what many experience when they receive feedback. It may not be far from the image you immediately conjure up when we simply mention the words *candor* and *feedback*. Honest, candid feedback, well delivered and frequently offered, creates a very different outcome.

A leader who is exceptional at providing coaching and feedback provides verbal feedback frequently and written feedback once or twice a year. The feedback should include genuine affirmation, as well as pointers on ways to grow and improve. As Larry Bossidy demonstrated, a one- or two-page memo should lay out the evaluator's assessment of the individual's performance, in terms of business results, values, and behaviors. It assesses how well the individual executed against agreed-on goals and lays out goals and actions for the coming year.

Ideally, a feedback session should be candid but not defeating, objective but not dispassionate, and instructive but not prescriptive. The conversation should include a heavy dose of affirmation, particularly at the end. As Goethe, the German poet and dramatist, said so well, "Encouragement after censure is as the sun after a shower."

Everyone has development needs

Under CEO Kevin Sharer, Amgen's managers have learned that everyone has developmental needs that should be addressed. In fact, when Sharer was tapped for the CEO job in May 2000, he conducted thirty-minute interviews with each of his top 140 people. One of the five questions he asked was, "What advice do you have for me?" He listened for seventy-five hours to their replies. At the end, he summarized all the verbal critiques and acknowledged that his most important development need was, ironically, to become a better listener.

That wasn't the only advice Sharer accepted. Once when he was conducting a leadership question-and-answer session, Sharer replied sharply to an employee who stood up to disagree with him. The incident chilled the room. Later, Ilana Meskin, Senior Director of Human Resources, left Sharer a voice mail message. "You have a way of shutting down the conversation that makes people not want to keep going," she said. "You defeat the very sort of exchange of ideas that you're seeking. The only way we'll achieve the benefit of 'best idea wins' is to open up, not shut down, the conversation."

Meskin got no reply. "I was walking around thinking my career was over," she noted. But at the next session, Sharer was a completely different person. The Q-and-A went on and on, with Sharer listening intently and replying with respect. Afterward, the session's facilitator came up to Sharer. "That was awesome," she said. Sharer turned and winked at Meskin. "I've been coached," he said with a smile.

By setting himself up as a model, Sharer has been able to instill the idea that everyone benefits from development. He has shown that to have a talent mindset that embraces development, senior leaders can't excuse themselves from that process.

In his annual discussions with his direct reports, Sharer sits down and writes a single paragraph about the person. "It's three or four sentences," he explains, "and then I say, 'Here are behaviors that are really working well, keep it up. Here are three things you need to change.' And that's all there are—those three things." Sharer acknowledges the process is simple, but he stresses that the important part is to set himself up as a coach, not a judge.

Making feedback and coaching happen

How can you make your company as open to coaching and feedback as Amgen has? Evolve toward a culture that consciously values feedback and coaching. Provide training where leaders can practice providing feedback and coaching to subordinates in role-playing situations. Add coaching and effective feedback to the key competencies you require in leaders. Include people development in the criteria for leaders' evaluations. Recruit leaders who are good at affirming and coaching people. Let "people development" weigh heavily in your promotion decisions.

Finally, institute a 360-degree feedback process. Send surveys to people below and above an individual, as well as to their peers, asking them to evaluate the person on a set of competencies. You will see that 360-degree feedback can provide very useful insights into a person's strengths and development needs—without the sweaty palms that happen when someone receives feedback solely from his or her boss. Of course, it also provides input from subordinates, who have perhaps the best perspective on that person's leadership skills. Include in the 360-degree survey how well leaders are caring for and developing their people.

If you go the next step and share the 360-degree feedback with the individual's boss, then you get the additional benefit of having a valuable input on the individual's people leadership skills. You're probably wondering if sharing the feedback with the boss undermines the candor of the responses. In companies where candor is deeply rooted in the culture, this is not the case.

Remember, that "candid, insightful feedback" was rated very important by nearly all respondents in our surveys and was also one of the developmental factors that companies fell shortest on (see figure 5-1).

Make Deliberate Mentoring Happen

What is the mystique of the Marine Corps that causes it to lead all other U.S. military services in recruitment levels? With help from Madison Avenue, the Corps tersely presents itself as "The Few. The Proud." Throughout its 225-year history, the Marine Corps has made it clear that enlistment standards are tough. They telegraph this message in no uncertain terms: Give us a few months and we will change the way you think about yourself, your peers, and your life. Marines do two things for their country: "We win battles and make Marines."

Although many people may believe that the Marines foster an "eat nails, spit rust" culture, they are actually something quite different. They are an organization built on developing people into leaders, and mentoring is an important part of that development.

"As a leader, you are holding an umbrella and your job is to keep all the bureaucratic nonsense away from your little puppies who are working for you," Marine Colonel Robert E. Lee (no relation to the confederate general) explains. "Unfortunately, you are holding that umbrella while your puppies are sometimes urinating in your shoes. But they're your puppies, and if you look at it that way, you take the stuff that is coming down and protect them from it."

Lee knows a bit about that. About thirty years ago he was a midshipman in the Naval Academy. By his senior year, his grades had slipped so low that he was called before the academic board. There was a good chance he'd be thrown out of the school. Fortunately, there was a Marine captain there by the name of Thomas Draude who was Lee's company officer and liked what he saw—a kid with a lot of energy and a great attitude, although certainly unfocused. Draude intervened. "I sat down with Lee and said, 'Okay, here's the question. How badly do you want to be a Naval Academy graduate?'" Draude recalls.

When Lee replied that he wanted it badly, Draude decided to go to bat for him. He appeared before the board with Lee, and when the Academy's superintendent asked whether Lee had any chance of making it, Draude replied, "Admiral, absolutely. I'll stay on him. I'll guarantee he'll make it through." But that wasn't enough. The decision came back: Lee was discharged.

Draude was surprised, but undeterred. He asked for another hearing, and again he pleaded for Lee. Finally, the board excused Lee and asked Draude to speak with them in private. "We just don't think the kid has what it takes," was their consensus. "Gentlemen," Draude heard himself replying, "I know Bobby Lee is no Phi Beta Kappa, but he can sure as hell lead troops. And I think that is what this place is still supposed to be about. I've just returned from my third time in Vietnam and think I know something about combat, something about leading troops. I'm telling you, we can't allow Bobby Lee to get away from us."

The board relented, and Lee got a second chance. This time Draude and his new company officer rode him hard, making sure that he spent the necessary time studying. Lee didn't disappoint them—in fact, he was on the dean's list the next semester and graduated first in his class at the Basic School. "Captain Draude saw things in me I didn't even know I had," comments Lee today.

Lee eventually became the Commanding Officer of the Basic School, in charge of the leadership training that is mandatory for every Marine. When we interviewed him he was an assistant to Richard Danzig, the Secretary of the Navy under President Clinton.

The important point here is that Lee has now passed the mentoring torch down to others.

Two of the people he has mentored, for instance, are Dave Odom and his wife, Michelle Trusso, two of Lee's stars. Both are honors graduates of the Marine Corps's premiere professional school for captains—Amphibious Warfare School—and both were recently promoted to majors. Now they, too, have become part of the Marines legacy, mentoring other young Marines beneath them. "I feel as a captain that I have these kernels of learning I need to pass on to the lieutenants," says Trusso. "I'm privileged to be a part of a legacy that was passed to me, and now I must pass it on to others."

Odom recalls an incident that epitomizes the importance—and occasional surprise outcome—of mentoring. He says that he once had a young lieutenant under his command who had been slacking off in general and who topped it off by writing an awful order (which in the military is similar to a lawyer's brief or case study).

"The lieutenant was eating breakfast and the rest of the lieutenants had left," Odom recalls. "I said, 'Stay here a minute,' and dropped his order down on the table next to him. 'It's pathetic,' I said. 'You're clearly wasting your time and mine.' The young man responded, 'Sir, I knew I was off performance. I wanted to go to the Notre Dame football game this past weekend with my dad. I wrote the order in a half hour.'"

Odom read him the riot act, telling the young man that this wasn't college—this was the Marines and he was responsible for people's lives. "If you aren't giving this 24 and 7—and this isn't just the party line—the troops you are leading are not going to respect you. They're not going to listen to you. If you aren't making the very best decisions you can, and staying in charge, people will die."

Odom then gave the lieutenant a list of the things that he expected him to accomplish, and on which he would be evaluated. "If you don't meet them, my recommendation will be that you go back to Colonel Lee for separation from the Marine Corps," Odom said sternly. Then Odom got up and left, leaving the young man sitting, stunned.

Odom kept an eye on the young lieutenant from then on, but had no idea of the impact this intervention had until months later. "At graduation, the lieutenant walked up with an older man in a big overcoat," Odom recalls. "This is my dad," the young man said to Odom. Then he turned to his father and said, "Sir, this is the man who turned my life around."

The power of mentoring

The word *mentor* comes from Homer's *Odyssey*. Before embarking on his epic voyage, Odysseus entrusted the care of his only son, Telemachus, to Mentor, a family friend. Twenty years later, Odysseus returned to find that Telemachus was taught well—having completed his own odyssey to manhood.

Mentoring has remained with us ever since. A mentor's job is to nurture self-esteem—not just by heaping praise, but by offering encouragement and by believing in the ability of the individual to achieve uncommonly great things. "A mentor sometimes gives you painful feedback in a way that's delivered with deep caring," explains Catherine Buck, a manager at Amgen's Boulder, Colorado facility. "A mentor helps you get back in the game. They say, 'You can vent and get through the hurt and defensiveness; I'll keep it all confidential. Then I'm going to give you some feedback and some advice—because you might not be seeing the big picture. I am giving you this because I want you to succeed.'"

Our research demonstrates the enormous power of mentoring. Of those respondents that have had a highly helpful mentoring experience, 95 percent said the experience motivated them to do their very best, 88 percent said the experience made them less likely to leave their company, and 97 percent said the experience contributed to their success at the company.[16] In one study we conducted with thirty-five people who had experienced real mentors, half of them said the mentoring experience "changed their life."[17] Those are powerful words.

Despite its powerful effect, though, mentoring is not understood, valued, or delivered in most companies. Only 47 percent of our respondents believed their company both values and recognizes the importance of mentoring, and only 25 percent said their company has formal systems to support or encourage mentoring relationships.[18]

Institutionalizing mentoring

In most companies, mentoring of some kind happens every day. By and large, though, it is a lucky occurrence for those few who happen to find someone with whom they have an affinity. Few organizations have mentoring deeply embedded in their cultures as the Marines have. In these rare cases, it's a heritage of mentoring that is passed from generation to generation. But how can the majority of companies that don't have such a rich heritage *make* mentoring happen?

To our surprise, we have found that good mentoring can be achieved through a deliberate effort. Some companies explicitly assign high-potential young people to more senior people and state expectations for that relationship such as the frequency of meetings and the topics they might discuss. Other companies simply encourage it by measuring it and by including mentoring in the overall evaluation of leaders. They ask people to name the individuals whom they consider to be mentors. Counting the number of mentees per leader reveals who are active mentors and who are not. Above all, these companies demonstrate that mentoring is valued.

Can you really institutionalize mentoring? That was the question that Arrow Electronics asked itself a few years ago: How can we bottle the passion, energy, and enhancement of loyalty that is born of informal mentoring and pass it around? How can we institutionalize the notion that leaders need to connect with people one at a time, and offer them encouragement, support, and fair-minded counsel?

Arrow found the answers to these questions and has acted on them. Arrow scored the highest of the thirty-five large companies participating in our survey on the question of mentoring, and *ComputerWorld* magazine named the company one of the best places for IT professionals to work. So how do they do it?

Carefully assign mentors. Arrow has a number of programs to formally assign mentors. The Worldwide Mentoring program, tailored for top managers, is one of the most important. The key to its success has been the centralized assignment process: Senior management carefully matches mentors and mentees. In fact, top leaders are specifically asked not to take on additional mentoring relationships on their own. "We might be planning to ask that person to mentor someone else—someone they don't even know," explains CEO Fran Scricco. "It may be someone who we think will be a higher return on the investment."

In addition to the process for choosing a mentor, many of the functions of the relationship are prescribed. For instance, Arrow explicitly states that the mentoring pairs should meet once a month and suggests topics that might be discussed. Rules of confidentiality are also laid out.

Mentors at Arrow take their responsibility quite seriously. B. J. Scheihing, Senior Vice President of Worldwide Operations, is one of the most sought-after mentors. "Mentoring is important enough to me that I build time for it into my calendar, including when I travel overseas," she says. "I once traveled from London to Denmark just to have dinner with someone I was mentoring. He couldn't believe the only reason for that leg of the trip was to spend time with him and I told him, 'You bet it is, and here's why: The next time you're having one of those days—when quitting seems like a pretty good idea—I want you to remember that you are important enough to Arrow that I made a special trip to Denmark to have dinner with you. Instead of quitting, I want you to pick up the phone and call me and together we'll figure out what to do.'"

Harriet Green, President of Arrow's Contract Manufacturing Services group, is equally vigilant about her six mentees. "I always have a marker somewhere in my Palm Pilot," she says, "so that if I haven't heard from one of my mentees, I will contact them." Green has regular breakfasts—preplanned a year in advance—with two of her mentees. For the other four, she uses the last Sunday of every month to remind herself to check up on them. "If we haven't been in touch, I send them a little note saying, 'Haven't heard from you. What's happening?'" She adds, "I use this structure to stay on track. Otherwise the mentee can say, 'Oh, well, mentoring never worked for me,' or the mentor will say, 'They never contacted me.' Both parties need to take responsibility in the process."

Each unit owns its own program. There isn't just one formal mentoring program at Arrow; there are many. Each unit is free to decide if and when it wants to start a mentoring program, and each has a fair bit of latitude about the exact design of the program.

Arrow's IT organization, for instance, has a mentoring program that launches ten to fifteen mentoring pairs twice each year. People looking for a mentor must do more than raise their hands. They must write down their goals and objectives for the program. They need to be clear about what they hope to get out of the relationship. This helps the mentoring steering committee determine a good fit with a mentor. Arrow found that people have different reasons for wanting a mentor, ranging from specific help with their jobs to the more frequent request for someone to teach them how to navigate their way around Arrow's complex organization.

Alan Napier, one of the IT unit's vice presidents, was a member of the IT department's first mentoring steering committee. "We spent a lot of time discussing the development needs of each person and trying to identify a mentor who would be just the right fit," he says. Sometimes that meant naming a mentor who had overcome a challenge that was now facing the mentee. In other cases, IT employees who needed business experience were assigned mentors from line organizations.

Arrow has learned that its mentoring programs deliver multiple benefits. First, they are a good way for the company to keep in touch with its key employees—who today are spread out across more than 225 sales offices and nineteen distribution centers in thirty-eight countries. Second, they give people in Arrow's far-flung offices a way to share personally in the company's values and leadership philosophy through their contact with other senior leaders.

"Finally," says Kathy Bernhard, Director of Management Development, "we realized that learning was reciprocal. Senior people wanted to do it because they got as much from the relationship as they gave to it."

That is certainly the case with Vinnie Vellucci, President of Arrow Bell Components. Vellucci has been active in mentoring relationships over his thirty-year Arrow career, both as a mentor and a mentee. "Some of the best feedback I've received in my career came from one of my mentors," he says. "While it stung at the time, I think I was more receptive to it from a mentor than I would have been from my boss. It's a funny thing, but you realize that your mentor has only one agenda—helping you succeed."

Mentoring at Amgen

Whereas Arrow Electronics has become a master at mentoring, Amgen is just beginning. Amgen CEO Kevin Sharer is leading the way by personally mentoring three of the company's high-potential vice presidents. He meets with each of them once a month and occasionally invites them to observe meetings or join him on business trips. "I'm trying to develop a leadership culture," he explains, "and mentoring is one way I'm doing it."

One of those whom Sharer mentors is Pam Hunt, Vice President of Research Therapeutics and a rising star in the company. "When Kevin decided he wanted to mentor me, he went to my boss to make sure there would be no problem. When my boss mentioned the possibility to me, I was flabbergasted. Just incredibly flattered," she says. Sharer called her into his office a week later and asked if this was something she was interested in. "Why would I say no?" she asks. "Kevin had done a lot of thinking about it. He had created a four-page mentoring plan that he pulled out of the drawer and showed to me—that was impressive."

From being around Sharer, Hunt has learned some invaluable lessons about the business. Equally important, though, she feels a deep sense of loyalty for a company that cares so much for her. "I don't think I could quit Amgen. The emotional ties are just too great," she says. "I look at my seventeen-year-old daughter and wish for her the success and joy that I've had in my career."

What about Training?

Earlier in this chapter, we said that training is not as important as job experience, coaching, and mentoring. It isn't. That said, it does play a role in developing leaders.

A 1992 report by A. T. Kearney estimated that 80 percent of all workplace training is not actually used on the job.[19] Although many of the criticisms have been, and continue to be, valid, we come not to bury training, but to praise it—at least the aspects of training that we believe are helpful to leadership development.

Two types of well-designed and well-delivered training can enhance managers' development: foundational managerial education and high-impact leadership development.

By *foundational managerial education*, we mean knowledge of management disciplines such as finance, operations, and marketing—the kinds of things that are taught in M.B.A. or executive education programs. This kind of training is particularly useful for more junior managers and for those facing transitions in their careers—for example, those moving into a managerial role for the first time.

The foundational education also includes training in general managerial skills, such as communications or interpersonal skills. To be effective, skills training should be immediately relevant, timely, high quality, and reinforced on the job. Although some skills are still best learned in face-to-face settings (e.g., presentation skills, giving and receiving feedback), many lend themselves to self-paced, technology-based solutions.

The second type of training—*leadership development training*—can *only* be delivered face-to-face, and the faces of the instructors should be those of well-respected senior leaders of the institution. The best leadership development programs are structured around action learning: solving real and important business problems. They should also include a large amount of high-quality feedback. Frequently, feedback on the trainee is solicited before the program from multiple people who have had different working relationships with the trainee. Then a third party synthesizes the responses and feeds it back. Some programs go one step further to observe the trainee over the course of the program and assess and provide feedback on his or her leadership style.

The best of these programs—such as GE's "Executive Development Course" at Crotonville, PepsiCo's "Building the Business," and Johnson & Johnson's "Taking Action on Issues"—bring together small groups of hand-picked, high-potential executives and put them to work with senior leaders to solve real business challenges. In one program, each team had to assess the attractiveness of the company's entering a particular country. They studied political and economic trends, and interviewed business and government leaders in the country. At the end of the month, the teams presented their findings to a group of senior executives, including the CEO, who then made binding decisions based on the team's recommendations.

Along the way, executives in these programs are introduced to new concepts, skills, and knowledge in a powerful, action-learning format. More important, however, they are immersed in the leadership principles and values of the organization. They develop strong, trust-based networks with their peers, internalize the culture of the organization, and begin to understand their role in shaping the culture going forward. They learn firsthand what it takes to be a successful leader in the organization. Many participants have described these programs as "life-shaping" events.

Although training does not equal—or even guarantee—learning, good training does contribute to the growth of leaders.

Raise Your Game

Is your company doing all that it can to grow great leaders? If you cannot answer "Yes" to the following questions, then your company has an opportunity to tune up its approach to leadership development.

- Does your company think expansively about the slate of candidates that could fill an opening? Do you ensure that your most talented people are placed in your most critical jobs? Do you consider who will grow most from serving in the role rather than simply looking for the person who has done it before and is most likely to be successful?

- Do you regularly provide candid feedback and coaching to your people that highlights their strengths and weaknesses and provides them useful guidance on where to focus their development energy?

- Do you openly value and encourage mentoring? Are you acting as mentor for two to four high-potential individuals and in doing so serving as a role model for others?

- Do you have a leadership training program that brings future leaders together with the senior executives in a way that inculcates the culture and values of the company, solves important business problems, and provides senior executives with exposure to the up-and-comers?

Developing people into leaders is both the privilege and responsibility of every leader. The *privilege* lies in seeing someone accomplish feats they never thought themselves capable of, tackle a new business challenge that seemed daunting at first, or succeed in a role that was intimidating at the outset. The *responsibility* lies in providing the development your people want, expect, and need to deliver better business results. Doing this well requires heart, soul, and real time, but your company's performance depends on it. It is that simple and that important.

Finally, it is important to remember that development is more than the sum of effective coaching, institutionalized mentoring, artful use of job rotation, and targeted training. As we witnessed in *Pygmalion*—and as you've undoubtedly experienced in your own maturation—development is a two-way process in which the teacher grows as much as the student. Development also depends as much on the individual's receptivity and initiative as it does on the organization's deliberate intentions.

Development is rarely linear since setbacks intermingle with advances. Development is also endless. We can never be as developed as we should be or would like to be. But that notion is expansive and hopeful, as captured by the words of an ancient sage, "If all the heavens were parchment, all human beings scribes, and all the trees of the forest pens, it would be insufficient to write what I have learnt from my teachers; and yet I only took away from them as much as a dog laps from the ocean."[20]

6

DIFFERENTIATE
AND AFFIRM
YOUR PEOPLE

The Battle of Britain began in the summer of 1940, when German pilots attacked from the skies, clearing the way for an invasion of Britain. England was caught unprepared: The Royal Air Force (RAF) did not have enough aircraft. Even worse, she didn't have enough pilots. To win, the British knew, they would have to shoot down the German planes at a rate of at least two to one.

To help turn the tide, the RAF broke its ranks of about 900 pilots into what they called A-class squadrons, B-class squadrons, and C-class squadrons. The A squadrons contained the very best flyers—pilots who knew how to command a flight, nurture fledgling pilots, and get their formations safely home. These pilots were drilled in the fast-changing tactics of the enemy and given permission to go for the most distant targets.

The B squadrons were less skilled in the air, but the RAF commanders continually encouraged and trained them. Despite the shortage of A-class fliers, the RAF always mixed some A fliers in with the B-class squadrons to serve as leaders and role models.

The C-class squadrons, on the other hand, were held on the ground as much as possible. Despite the need for more fliers, the

RAF realized that mixing C-level fliers into the furious attacks might kill as many of their own pilots as the Germans did.

Within months, the RAF had developed a skilled and highly motivated fighting force, and by November 1940, the pilots—none of whom, incidentally, was over the age of twenty-three—had thrown back the German air force.[1] It was Winston Churchill who uttered the now famous words, "Never in the field of human conflict was so much owed, by so many, to so few."

The war for talent, thankfully, lacks the fire and bloodshed of the Battle of Britain. Nevertheless, just as the RAF was able to accomplish the impossible by segmenting its fighting force, companies can achieve higher performance by differentiating between their high, average, and low performers. If more companies had the discipline and courage to differentiate their talent this way, they, too, could accomplish the impossible.

This chapter explores three important themes: why it is necessary to differentiate the people in your talent pool; why the counterbalancing measure—affirmation—is also required; and the ethical considerations that surround these difficult issues.

Furthermore, this chapter will show you how to invest in your most capable people (the A players), grow the solidly contributing middle (the B players), act decisively on the low performers (the C players), and put the spotlight on all three in a rigorous talent review process.

The Courage to Reshape Long-Standing Ethics

In the struggle to be fair and compassionate leaders, many would prefer to think of all colleagues as equally talented, and to treat them all the same. However, in reality, some people perform better than others.

Differentiation entails assessing the performance and potential of your people and then giving them the commensurate promotion, compensation, and development opportunities. It means investing in the A players, so you are sure to retain and develop them; affirming and developing the B players, so they can contribute their best; and acting decisively on the C players, either by helping them raise their performance or by removing them from critical positions. We are not discussing the D players—the clearly incompetent or unethical managers—since all companies take quick action on them.

What precisely do we mean by A, B, and C players? You could think of these three levels in *absolute* terms: A players define the standard for exceptional performance by consistently delivering results and inspiring and motivating others; B players are solid performers who meet expectations but who may have limited upward mobility; and C players deliver barely acceptable results. You could also think of them in *relative* terms: In a particular company, A players are the best 10 to 20 percent, B players are the middle 60 to 70 percent, and C players are the bottom 10 to 20 percent. Whichever approach you use for defining your talent segments, be sure to install a common definition that can be consistently applied.

Many companies are uncomfortable designating people as As, Bs, and Cs. Differentiation requires a willingness to acknowledge that among the many committed hard workers, some contribute more than others in terms of performance and impact to the organization.

At the core of this discomfort is a genuine ambivalence about passing judgment on people. However, it is important to remember that you are *not* passing judgment. You are assessing performance. Moreover, it is not a permanent verdict. In fact, the underlying purpose of the assessment is to help people improve their performance.

Critics of differentiation argue that it promotes a star culture that undermines teamwork. This doesn't have to be the case, however. Differentiating your As, Bs, and Cs doesn't mean that you are stamping a grade on their forehead. In fact, you may choose not to tell people what their current assessment is. Furthermore, it doesn't require that all of the performance rewards be based on individual performance. You could, for instance, base all or some of a manager's variable pay on team performance.

Other critics of differentiation argue that it takes universal praise to keep everyone motivated. We don't think this is true, either.

Ninety-four percent of the managers we surveyed said that recognition for their individual contributions is very important to them.[2]

There are some downsides to differentiation. The B players won't feel quite as attended to as the A players. There will be pain for the C players (and for the managers who must tell them that their performance is inadequate). But what is the alternative? Not investing the most important development opportunities in the people who have the highest likelihood of becoming leaders in your company? Not getting the top-flight players because you can't afford to pay them? Not putting your most talented people in your most critical jobs? Not being candid with people about their development needs so that they can work on them?

Imagine the excitement if your CEO announced that a midlevel engineer who was widely acclaimed to be a terrific leader was promoted to be head of product engineering for the entire corporation. Imagine your boss telling *you* that your performance was rated outstanding and handing you a 40 percent merit increase rather than the 4 percent you had expected. Imagine the buzz that would ring through your company if a long-tenured senior executive who had failed for years to provide inspirational leadership—in fact, who was a real demotivator—were asked to leave.

The enormous power of affirmation

Affirmation, on the other hand, means making people feel appreciated, recognized, and valued for their unique contributions. Affirmation helps drive an individual's performance and job satisfaction. People want and need to feel valued as a productive part of the institution. When they aren't, they become demoralized, they are more likely to leave the company, and their performance invariably suffers. As the philosopher and psychologist William James understood, "The deepest principle in human nature is the craving to be appreciated." Even C players need their self-worth affirmed—through recognition of the strengths they can leverage into another role.

In our research, two-thirds of respondents who were considering leaving their current employer cited "not feeling valued" as a reason for leaving (see figure 6-1). On the other hand, employees who feel affirmed by their companies said they are more satisfied with their jobs and less likely to leave.[3]

Differentiation and affirmation together form an ethic about how to manage people. For many companies this is quite different from the ethic they are accustomed to.

Figure 6-1 Not Feeling Valued Is a Big Reason Why People Leave

% of all respondents who said critical or very important

Is there a greater than 30 percent chance you will leave this company in the next two years? If so, why?

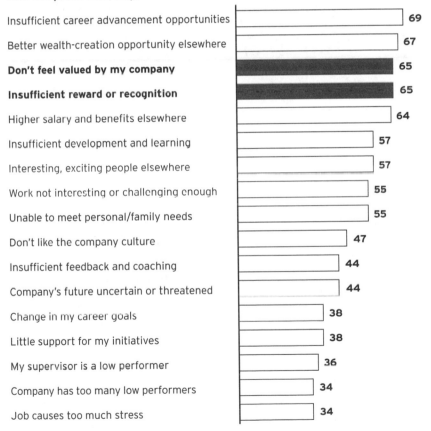

Insufficient career advancement opportunities	69
Better wealth-creation opportunity elsewhere	67
Don't feel valued by my company	65
Insufficient reward or recognition	65
Higher salary and benefits elsewhere	64
Insufficient development and learning	57
Interesting, exciting people elsewhere	57
Work not interesting or challenging enough	55
Unable to meet personal/family needs	55
Don't like the company culture	47
Insufficient feedback and coaching	44
Company's future uncertain or threatened	44
Change in my career goals	38
Little support for my initiatives	38
My supervisor is a low performer	36
Company has too many low performers	34
Job causes too much stress	34

Source: McKinsey & Company's War for Talent 2000 Survey, middle and senior managers

The Old Ethics	The New Ethics
We invest in all our people equally	Some people are more talented and perform much better than others, and we invest in them accordingly
We give best performers a little more money than average performers	We give best performers a lot more money
I know Charlie's a C player, but we have to be fair to him— he's been here fifteen years	We have to be fair to the twenty people working under Charlie
Managers don't need pats on the back	Managers, like everyone else, need to know they are valued
Ethical managers don't talk about others behind their backs	Managers have a responsibility to discuss the people in their organization
Undifferentiated praise motivates the masses	Differentiation drives individual and company performance

Invest Heavily in the A Players

Bill Boyle, Director of Experimental Biology at Amgen, knows the value of A-class talent. Several years ago, Amgen was racing against several competitors to develop a new anemia-fighting drug to help dialysis patients. "We had great people working around the clock on it. In the end we beat the competition for the Epogen patent by just a few days," he says. What was the difference that that team of high performers made? This year, Amgen's Epogen market is about $2 billion worldwide and growing. If you multiply that number by the total lifespan of the drug, it amounts to something on the magnitude of a $50 billion opportunity. "The scientists who pushed that product forward were among the best in the industry—the top layer," he says. "Their efforts created this extraordinary opportunity for Amgen."

There's no doubt that A players boost company performance. Because they create the most shareholder value, either directly or through their ability to inspire and motivate others, you should invest in them accordingly. The high-performing companies do this, as shown in figure 6-2. To make sure highly talented people stay with your company, you need to do everything you can to keep them engaged and satisfied—even delighted.

Find out what they would most like to be doing, and shape their career and responsibilities in that direction. Solve any issues that might be pushing them out the door, such as a boss that frustrates them or travel demands that burden them. Consider assigning a mentor to each A player, not only to help that person develop, but also to help resolve any problems that might cause him or her to leave the company one day.

You need to accelerate the development of your A players as much as possible, both to help retain them and to maximize their ability to contribute to the company. A players need challenging jobs that will stretch their abilities. You might think that most campanies would do this, yet only 23 percent of the managers in

Figure 6-2 Identify and Invest in A Players

% of corporate officers who strongly agree

Source: McKinsey & Company's War for Talent 2000 Survey

our survey strongly agreed that their company gives high performers better and faster development opportunities than average performers.[4]

Make sure A players regularly receive candid, affirming dialogue about their strengths and development needs. Provide constructive, energizing coaching and assign one of your best mentors
to them. Because such mentors are scarce, make sure they are
spending their time where it has the most development leverage.

Differentiating development opportunities is not enough. You
must also differentiate compensation. Unfortunately, most companies
don't do enough for their A players. In our survey, only 15 percent
of managers strongly agreed that high performers in their company
make at least 20 percent more money than average performers.[5]

The traditional philosophy of internal equity—paying everyone
doing the same job the same amount of money—is giving way to a
new sense of equity, which dictates that you should pay people relative to the value they create. In fact, the corporate officers in our
survey believe that top performers should be paid on average 42
percent more than average performers.[6]

Surprisingly, most companies do not pay top performers in the
same salary grade much more than average performers. In some
cases where we have done this analysis, the difference in total compensation paid is as little as 10 percent.

Paying the A players more doesn't have to create competition
between people, and it doesn't have to create a star culture. The
degree of the differentiation and the mix of individual and team-based
incentives will determine whether you create a more team-based
culture or a more individual-based culture. For example, a more
team-based model might include sizable differences in *salaries*
(depending on the individual's talents and contributions) while bas-
ing the *incentive pay* on team or company performance. Each company will have to determine what is suitable for its situation.

Overall, it is important to remember that A players need as
much attention as the Bs and Cs. "Conventional wisdom is, 'You've
got some great people working for you. So you don't have to worry

about them,'" explains U.S. Marine Colonel Robert E. Lee. "But rising stars are more demanding to lead. They're more needy of your leadership. They question you all the time, constantly think about things, and are always coming up with ideas. They challenge you! But that's how your best leaders grow, and if you don't spend time with your best people, you're going to lose them."

That's the lesson that Hewlett-Packard and Procter & Gamble learned when they analyzed their "regretted losses": Many of the people who left did not know how highly regarded they were by the company's leaders.[7] That's a regrettable way to lose talent.

Grow the Solidly Contributing B Players

In your effort to invest in the A players, don't overlook the next 60 to 70 percent of your talent pool—the individuals who keep the business running day after day—the solid B players. They may not stand out like the As, but without them your company would be paralyzed. You can't build a talent pool with A players alone.

"A true talent mindset cuts across the organization," Amgen's HR leader Ilana Meskin reminds us. "It's about spending your capital on strong contributors from all parts of the organization—those who exhibit learning agility and those who just seem ready and eager to grow. They're the ones who will benefit the most from the investment and from whom the organization will gain the greatest rewards." She added, "My greatest hope is that development and affirmation will not solely be lavished on superstars, but generously showered on core contributors throughout the entire organization."

With B players, the object is to increase their capabilities, energize them, and retain them with appropriate investment. You need to develop your Bs and affirm them.

Developing the B players will improve their productivity and satisfaction, and help some of them become A players. Encourage them, stretch them, and from time to time assess them to see if they have advanced. What is the value of having all your average-performing sales representatives increase their annual revenue by 3 percentage points? Or your plant managers increase real productivity from 2 percent to 4 percent a year? Obviously, the value creation potential is considerable.

So make sure the B players get the development they need. Give them helpful, honest feedback and coaching. Affirm their strengths, be candid about their shortcomings, and coach them. Some will have the motivation and capability to grow. Letting them know where they stand is the first step in helping them move their game up a notch. Show your faith in them by challenging them and giving them ever greater responsibilities. The watchword for a Catholic monastery, Conception Abbey, offers an inspiring thought about this: "The violets in the mountain can break rocks if we believe in them and watch them grow."[8]

You also have to make a deliberate effort to affirm the B players—to let them know they are valued and that their contributions are recognized. Admittedly, giving A players more opportunities and more pay does run some risk of making the B players feel less satisfied and less motivated. The affirming actions listed here, however, will help motivate and inspire your solid contributors, and should help offset any potential downside.

- Show genuine interest and caring for your people and tell them they are valued. Tell them how you feel about them. Don't lose them because you didn't tell them they were important to the company. "I think it boils down to a very simple principle: You've got to have a leadership team that really cares about people and their careers," says Georgia-Pacific's Steve Macadam. "And trust me, you can't fake caring."

- Listen carefully and attentively to what they have to say. Internalize it, and respond thoughtfully and respectfully. Listening to people and acting on their suggestions affirms their sense of worth. As Steve Kaufman, former CEO and now Chairman of Arrow Electronics, says, "I had to learn to listen with my ears, not my mouth." Most companies fall short of this, but the problem can be addressed. Breakfast, lunch, coffee, town-hall meetings, hallway conversations—any of these will help. Talk to your people and listen nondefensively to what they have to say.

- Praise their distinctive strengths. Look for the things that individuals are particularly good at and tell them—and others—how much you appreciate that particular strength. Greg Summe at PerkinElmer is particularly good at this. One manager who worked for him commented, "Greg would sing your praises in front of others and make you feel like a star. He did this for everyone. This made you feel so good about yourself. When later on he told you the three things you needed to do to improve your performance, it was easier to take."

- Recognize their accomplishments with new opportunities. Placing your people in jobs that are congruent with their professional growth needs communicates your recognition of their work and your hope that they can contribute even more. There are other ways to show appreciation, as well. Arrow Electronics, for instance, sends about fifty of its managers each year to Harvard Business School for three days of training featuring lectures by professors and sessions with Arrow's top leaders. About one-third of the participants are Arrow's A players, but the rest are promising B players. For the A players, the message is that they will soon be leaders and they are valued. For the Bs, the message is that they're performing well, their contribution to the company is appreciated, and the company believes they have more potential.

- Trust them. Demonstrate your trust through your words and actions. Give them room to make decisions and take actions that are consistent with their potential. Openly share information about the business so that their decisions are fully informed.

- Pay them well for their contributions. Do you have productive salespeople who nevertheless won't become sales managers? If so, rate these types of people as B players, and make sure that their compensation is commensurate with their contributions.

Act Decisively on C Players

A C player is typically someone who delivers only minimally acceptable results. C players think incrementally and rarely create something bold or innovative. They rarely inspire. No one clamors to work with them and no one learns very much from them.

C players aren't bad people. Many have worked hard during their time with the company and have tried their best. Some may have been strong performers in the past, but the pace of change has left them behind with skills that are no longer sufficient. They may have been an A or B player in another role.

Everyone knows who the underperforming managers are in their companies. Everyone knows they don't deliver and everyone knows they hold the rest of the team back.

With C players, the objective is to help them become Bs (or even As) or, alternatively, to move them out of their jobs. In some cases this means helping them raise their game. In others, it means moving them to a different position where they can be successful, even shine. In still other cases, it means asking them to leave the company.

The enormous hidden cost of Cs

When C players are kept in leadership positions, they cost the company and the people who work under them an enormous amount. Although the emotional pain and management time associated with moving underperformers aside can be considerable—and we do not trivialize them—the hidden costs of *not* moving them are even greater.

C performers make bad bosses. Fifty-eight percent of respondents in our surveys said they have worked for an underperforming boss. About 80 percent of them said the experience prevented them from learning, hurt their career, and prevented them from making a greater contribution to the bottom line. A full 85 percent said it made them want to leave the company.[9] As figure 6-3 indicates, keeping C players perpetuates a vicious cycle. Bosses who are C players don't develop their subordinates, don't serve as good role models or coaches, and don't boost the productivity and morale of the people around them.

C players also tend to attract other C players. Netscape co-founder Marc Andreessen put it bluntly: "We hired very fast at Netscape and ended up with some groups filled with supergeniuses and others that weren't. It was very dependent on who the managers were. If you hired the right manager, that particular group was going to be great. But if you happened to hire a bad manager, that whole place was going to be horrible. We call it the Rule of Crappy People: Bad managers hire very, very bad employees, because they're threatened by anybody who is anywhere as good as they are."[10]

When leaders don't move on poor performers, it makes the other employees feel that the company is being poorly managed.[11] The perception of how well the company is managed is a critical element of an EVP and a driver of job satisfaction.

Finally, there is also the direct opportunity cost of having a C player in a job instead of an A player. Managers who are A players create much more value for the company than C players do—80 to 130 percent more value in the cases we have studied.[12] Replacing even half of your C players with A players would have a substantial impact on the performance of your organization.

Figure 6-3 Keeping C Players Perpetuates a Vicious Cycle

Why isn't there more movement?

Almost everyone wants the company to do something about low performers, but most companies don't (see figure 6-4).

Executives and managers cite many reasons for not acting on underperformers. Some say they aren't sure enough about their own ability to form judgments about other people. Some have doubts about their own skills and are fearful that criticizing others exposes them to criticism, too. Some think that anyone can be developed. Others say that it is disrespectful to the person. Some fear they won't be able to find a better replacement. Still others fear legal action.

All of these are real issues, but they are not the greatest obstacle. According to our research, the primary reason for inaction is that managers are unwilling to fire or move aside people who have contributed to the company and "met expectations" in the past, or people with whom they have been working for many years.[13] Yet high-performing companies take more action on C players, as figure 6-5 shows.

Figure 6-4 Not Enough Action on C Players

% of middle and senior managers

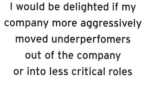
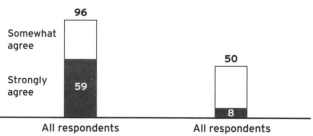

I would be delighted if my company more aggressively moved underperfomers out of the company or into less critical roles	Our company is actively moving underperformers out of the company or into less critical roles

Somewhat agree

96

Strongly agree — 59

50

8

All respondents   All respondents

Source: McKinsey & Company's War for Talent 2000 Survey

Figure 6-5   Take Action on C Players

% of corporate officers and senior managers

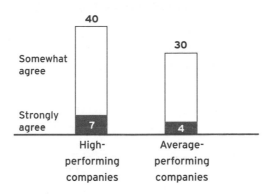

We regularly move C players to
continuously upgrade our talent pool

Source: McKinsey & Company's War for Talent 2000 Survey

It is very painful to deliver bad news to people who have been loyal colleagues or friends for a long time. Understandably, people are concerned about being "fair" to the individual involved. They say to themselves, "Let's be fair to Charlie. He's been with us for fifteen years." However, they should also consider this: "Let's be fair to the twenty talented people under Charlie—and move Charlie out or aside."

As Debra Dunn, a senior general manager at Hewlett-Packard, told us several years ago, "I feel there is no greater disrespect you can do to a person than to let them hang out in a job where they are not respected by their peers, not viewed as successful, and probably losing their self-esteem. To do that under the guise of respect for people is, to me, ridiculous."

Because it is painful and emotionally trying to deal with C players, many leaders become paralyzed when attempting to do so. A recent study published in *Fortune* magazine noted that the single greatest reason for the failure of CEOs is their inability to deal with their own poorly performing subordinates. As one CEO admitted, "It was staring me in the face but I refused to see it." Authors Charan and Colvin summarized, "The failure is one of emotional strength."[14]

Two ways to do it

What's the best way to move on C players? At GE, AlliedSignal, PerkinElmer, and the Marine Corps, underperformers are given ample time to raise their game after feedback and coaching. If they don't adequately respond, leaders develop a transition plan for the C players' exit from the company. These companies believe their businesses move too quickly for these people to catch up and keep up, and they don't believe in shunting those people to other jobs within the company. They also believe that the sooner in one's career that performance issues are addressed, the better for all concerned. They see it as the most compassionate approach in the long run.

For other companies, including Intel, Arrow Electronics, and The Home Depot, an underperformer who was once a top performer will first be moved laterally or back a level, where they can at least be an average performer. At The Home Depot, for instance, district managers who are struggling might be moved back to the position of store manager—where, indeed, half become successful again. For those who continue to be unsuccessful, the company will eventually ask them to leave.

At Arrow, every effort is made to help underperformers find a more appropriate job where they can still add real value to the company. Alan Napier, Vice President of Information Technology, believes that most people really want to do a good job and it's management's role to find a place that fits them. Says Napier, "When somebody is honestly trying to do something with everything they have and still failing, I don't think any less of that person. Almost always they're just in the wrong role. I spend a lot of time talking with my people and getting to know them, so when they're floundering, I can usually help them. We'll sit down in my office and try to figure out a better situation for them within Arrow. After our discussion we'll walk out of my office, both smiling, because that person is actually relieved. They feel the pressure incredibly, too."

Of course, there are limits to how many people you can demote or move aside, and it has to be done delicately. Demoting managers has to be done in a way that preserves their dignity. When The Home Depot moves district managers back to store managers, for instance, they usually move them to a new district where their stumble may have gone unnoticed.

You also have to know when it is time to call it quits. PerkinElmer CEO Greg Summe says there have been times when he realized that he had spent too much time trying to rehabilitate a low performer. "Every time I made a personnel change, I wished I had made it sooner," he said.

Iron hand in a velvet glove

Taking decisive action on C players requires an iron hand *and* a velvet glove.[15] Without an iron hand, leaders are inclined to avoid taking this difficult action. Without the velvet glove, the process can be insensitive and disrespectful, which can erode morale and make managers even less inclined to act.

The following actions ensure the iron hand:

- Require managers to identify and deal with C players. No one likes to deal directly with a poor performer. It is much easier to tolerate a low performer or move that person to another department, even if he or she struggles there, too.

- Make sure several senior people contribute to the assessment of low performers. This ensures a more accurate assessment and bolsters the confidence and resolve of the direct boss.

- Move managers around fairly frequently. A new manager will see people with fresh eyes and will find it easier to take action on low performers if he or she isn't as emotionally close to them.

- Teach line managers how to manage poor performers. This could be handled as a part of formal training that managers receive when they transition into managerial roles, or it could come in the form of coaching provided by superiors or HR managers during specific incidents.

These actions ensure the velvet glove:

- Provide individuals with regular, candid feedback. The decision to move someone out or aside should never come as a surprise to that person. The individual should receive multiple sessions of candid feedback, formal written feedback once a year, and continuous discussion along the way. Doing this ensures that they at least understand the assessment, even if they don't agree with it.

- Give people time while still in their current position to find their next job, whether that be inside or outside the company. When the new position is settled, the person can then announce his or her departure in the context of the new opportunity.

- Provide counsel (both career counsel and personal counsel) to help people navigate through the transition with dignity and with their self-esteem as intact as possible.

- Ease the financial transition. Companies that provide generous severance packages mitigate some of the ill feelings and much of the near-term financial burden associated with the separation.

Of course, there are legal risks involved in firing anyone. You should manage those risks but not try to eliminate them entirely. Seek counsel from HR managers and lawyers to ensure the process is objective and unbiased. Tie the receipt of severance to an agreement not to sue. Make sure the HR department understands that it is its role to facilitate, not block, the removal of low performers. HR should remind leaders of the action plans they committed to, counsel them on how to conduct the process, and arrange access to severance and outplacement services.

Finally, when your resolve seems to falter, remember all the struggling employees you inherited from your predecessors and commit to never leaving underperformers for *your* successors.

Wexner's totem poles

Les Wexner, CEO of The Limited, struggled with the ethical issues when dealing with his C players. Wexner decided to sort his players into thirds, or *totem pole* the people who reported directly to him. "I asked myself, 'Do I really want to do this? Is this humane, and is this fair?'" Wexner recalls. "All people are, after all, created equal. How can I have A, B, and Cs—top tier, middle tier, and bottom tier? Decisions around their careers and responsibility to their families—those are the toughest issues, particularly if they are negative decisions."

Wexner pondered these issues with a fair amount of unease and finally found some clarity and consolation. "When you take on a leadership role, you make these kinds of decisions on a moral basis," he explained. "Whether you are in the public sector or the private sector, you have a responsibility as a stakeholder. Morally, I would argue that if I don't make the tough decisions about the people who are preventing the enterprise from being successful, then I am putting at risk 150,000 or 175,000 people who are depending on that leadership. To me, the morality of leading the war for talent is this: If you don't lead the war for talent, you will be the victim in the war for talent."

Once Wexner overcame these difficult ethical issues, he had to decide what actions to take. "My first decision was to look at the bottom tier and say, 'Is this a developmental issue? Is this a values issue? Is it a skills/talent issue?'" he says. "For most of the people in the bottom tier, the judgment was: hopeless. Making that list helped me see that some of the people in the middle tier had strong potential. For example, this person is a certifiable talent—but they haven't for some reason gotten the development they need."

Wexner believes that you have to sincerely care for the people you are responsible for. People have to feel that caring in a realistic way. "You have to tell the whole truth about how you view them," he explains. "I think it is easy to be a bad leader, because bad leaders believe in utopias. Everyone is beautiful. Everyone is going to be promoted. The share price will increase 130 percent forever. By contrast, a good leader offers consistency and a balanced view. It comes back to the decisions you make in the war for talent. You have to constantly accept that the world is changing. Suddenly you're making the right moral judgment and it isn't about greed and pain or even business judgment. It is about responsibility to all your people."

Run a Robust Talent Review Process

Differentiating and affirming your people relies on insightful, robust assessments of them. This is not a book about HR processes, but there is one process you must have: a robust talent review. An effective talent review process is the spine of excellent talent management.

The talent review process is so important that we are going to describe it in some detail—the purpose, the players, the feel of it, and the outcomes. An effective talent review process is as fundamental to a well-managed company as is an effective budget process. But most companies are not close to having the kind of talent review they should. A sound process should assess your people against appropriately high standards of leadership excellence. It should serve as the basis for allocating opportunities, compensation, and further development, and it should allow the company's leaders to discover the depths and weaknesses of each unit's talent pool.

The talent review process is not the same as a traditional performance evaluation—the process that occurs annually between the boss and the subordinate. Rather, in a talent review process a leadership team looks at each unit's talent pool in order to identify the highest and lowest performers and to decide how to strengthen the organization.

Traditional succession planning is ineffective

Most companies have a succession planning process, but in most cases it is ineffective. The division presidents and the top HR officers typically go to headquarters once a year for half a day. They present color-coded charts of backups for various positions. They discuss possible successors and take turns presenting their charts.

The proceedings have an air of civility. All too often, no one asks tough questions or challenges the presenter because they don't know the people spoken about, the probability of those people ever moving to their division is low, or disagreement might seem impolite. Overall, the session lacks candor and yields names of successors who frequently are not suitable for filling a vacancy.

There are three fundamental differences between traditional succession planning and a robust talent review. First, a robust talent review is a full-day meeting held at each division chaired by the CEO and senior vice president of HR. They meet with the division president first to discuss the executive team and then meet with the full executive team to discuss their direct reports. By the end of the day, they will have discussed more than 50 managers and a number of up-and-coming, high-potential people.

Second, the talent review is both a name-by-name discussion of individuals and an assessment of the strength of the talent pool

Traditional Succession Planning	Robust Talent Review
A half-day session once a year at corporate headquarters	A full day on-site for each division
Discuss possible successors	Discuss quality of incumbents
Review individuals	Review individuals and the talent strength of each unit, and discuss other issues such as retention or recruiting
Polite, senatorial presentations	Rigorous, candid debate
No effort to calibrate assessments	Drive to a distribution of ratings
No action plans agreed to	Specific action plans written and followed up for each unit
An annual paper exercise	As important and intense as the budget process, with real accountability and a performance focus

Figure 6-6   Distinctive Elements of an Effective Talent Review

% of corporate officers who strongly agree

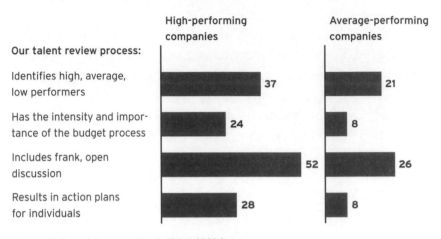

Source: McKinsey & Company's War for Talent 2000 Survey

overall in that division. The participants discuss the talent strength of each function and each region, and they discuss any overarching issues such as diversity, recruiting requirements, or retention—all in the context of that unit's business objectives.

Finally, the meeting has intensity and clarity of purpose around strengthening the talent pool to drive business performance. Discussions are open and candid and result in plans explicitly intended to take action at the individual and unit levels. Participants make the tough calls on people in a decisive, timely, and respectful way.

Figure 6-6 shows some of the critical features of an effective talent review process and how much better the high-performing companies perform them.

When pushed to the extreme, the purpose of the talent review is not to review people, rate them, or place them in charts, although these things do happen. The purpose is to drive the company well past business-as-usual and performance-as-expected by finding people who will do jobs in ways that they have never been done in the past. It's to look for extraordinary, counterintuitive moves for people, recognizing the value that talented people can create and pushing people to their limits. It's to generate confidence and enthusiasm around a set of decisions and actions about the deployment and development of people that have the potential to take the business to new heights. It's about building a pool of managerial talent stronger than one's competitors. It's about winning in the market. It's about performance.

Imagine a talent review that has the intensity of a rigorous budget review, unlike anything most companies have ever had in their HR processes. Try to imagine the intensity and single-minded focus on performance in the room during a robust talent review. Imagine what a robust talent review like this could do for your company.

The required elements of a talent review process

The talent review is designed to impact two fronts: the individual level and the organization unit level. The details of the talent review process will vary from company to company, but there are several elements that every talent review process should include.

1. Start with the business strategy. Open the meeting with an overview of your business objectives and a hard-driving discussion of the most pressing talent issues that stand in the way of the business meeting and its performance goals. Some 79 percent of corporate officers in the War For Talent Survey strongly agreed there should be a tight link between business strategy and talent pool requirements, but only 10 percent strongly agreed that this happens.[16] The purpose of the talent review is to figure out the talent required to deliver the business strategy and to constantly strengthen the talent pool.

2. Rigorously assess each individual. Discuss the performance and potential of each individual, name by name. Identify their strengths, weaknesses, and development needs. Assess each individual against a gold standard for top performance. This standard should include the competencies and values that are required of leaders in this organization, and should outline the behaviors that characterize high, average, and poor performance for each of them. This provides common language for the discussion and objective criteria for the assessment.

Facilitate a candid, probing, no-holds-barred debate about each individual. Pay particular attention to the As and the Cs, as well as to the people about whom there is a difference of opinion.

There should be at least two or three people in the room who know each individual well enough to be able to contribute to the assessment discussion. If this isn't the case, orchestrate ways to make this happen before the next review process. As important as good assessment is, it's impossible to make it perfectly objective. Although facts and objective criteria should be brought to bear, assessing people ultimately depends on good judgment and even some subjectivity. The best way to improve the quality of the assessment is to combine the viewpoints of several people.

3. Drive to a meaningful segmentation of performance. Post the names of the forty to sixty people being discussed on a segmentation scheme, forcing yourself to identify the As, Bs, and Cs. The segmentation can be based on quintiles, a normal distribution, or other predetermined percentages that differentiate the talent pool into meaningfully sized categories. Work with a large enough sample (more than forty people) to ensure a fairly normal distribution. Force some form of distribution of people across the categories. But don't try to precisely rank each individual—you will get bogged down in a nonproductive debate about whether a person is ranked at number 23 or 24. It's the reasonable distribution across three to five buckets of ratings that matters.

Use a very simple assessment tool—the simpler the better. Customize the tool to your particular needs. One effective tool is the performance/potential grid shown in figure 6-7. When each business unit uses a common standard for assessing talent and drives toward a common distribution of ratings, the company can calibrate assessments across the organization.

Figure 6-7 Performance/Potential Grid

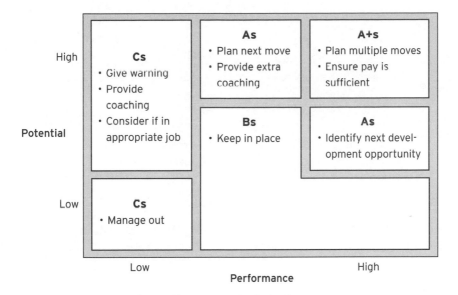

Another option is a grid that plots results on one axis and the company's values on the other. You could customize your own, as Sun-Trust Banks did. They put their top 200 into one of four buckets: large market growers, small market growers, maintainers, or strugglers.

4. Write action plans for each individual. After assessing each individual, decide on the specific actions you will take. The objective here is to make sure real consequences for people's careers result from the discussions. You don't need to have a lengthy development plan for each individual, but you do need to capture the two to five agreed-on actions. Figure 6-8 illustrates a range of sample actions that could be decided in the talent review. Take immediate action steps where appropriate.

5. Assess each unit's overall talent strength and write action plans at the unit level. After the individuals have been assessed, discuss the overall talent strength of the unit. How strong is each function? Each region? What talent issues are there that hold the unit back?

Figure 6-8 Write an Action Plan for Each Individual

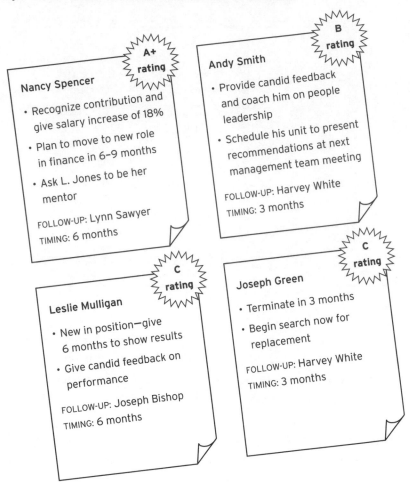

Nancy Spencer
A+ rating

- Recognize contribution and give salary increase of 18%
- Plan to move to new role in finance in 6–9 months
- Ask L. Jones to be her mentor

FOLLOW-UP: Lynn Sawyer
TIMING: 6 months

Andy Smith
B rating

- Provide candid feedback and coach him on people leadership
- Schedule his unit to present recommendations at next management team meeting

FOLLOW-UP: Harvey White
TIMING: 3 months

Leslie Mulligan
C rating

- New in position—give 6 months to show results
- Give candid feedback on performance

FOLLOW-UP: Joseph Bishop
TIMING: 6 months

Joseph Green
C rating

- Terminate in 3 months
- Begin search now for replacement

FOLLOW-UP: Harvey White
TIMING: 3 months

How well or poorly is the unit recruiting, developing, and retaining top performers? Moving on underperformers? Are there any issues such as diversity or low scores on employee surveys to discuss? Agree on a set of actions that will be taken to strengthen the unit's talent pool over the coming year. This should include some summary-level actions that result from the individual assessments, such as "Hire two people in at the vice president level," "Replace five low performers," or "Make two cross-divisional moves happen." It should also include actions to be taken on broader issues such as strengthening the EVP, strengthening a function, developing new recruiting strategies, and implementing retention tactics, to name a few.

At the end of the talent review, write a hard-hitting, three- to five-page plan that lists specific actions the unit will take to shore up weaknesses (see figure 6-9).

6. Accountability and follow-up. Holding leaders accountable for delivering the action plan is essential. Each leader must assess whether she or he has accomplished the commitments quarterly

Figure 6-9 Write an Action Plan for Each Unit

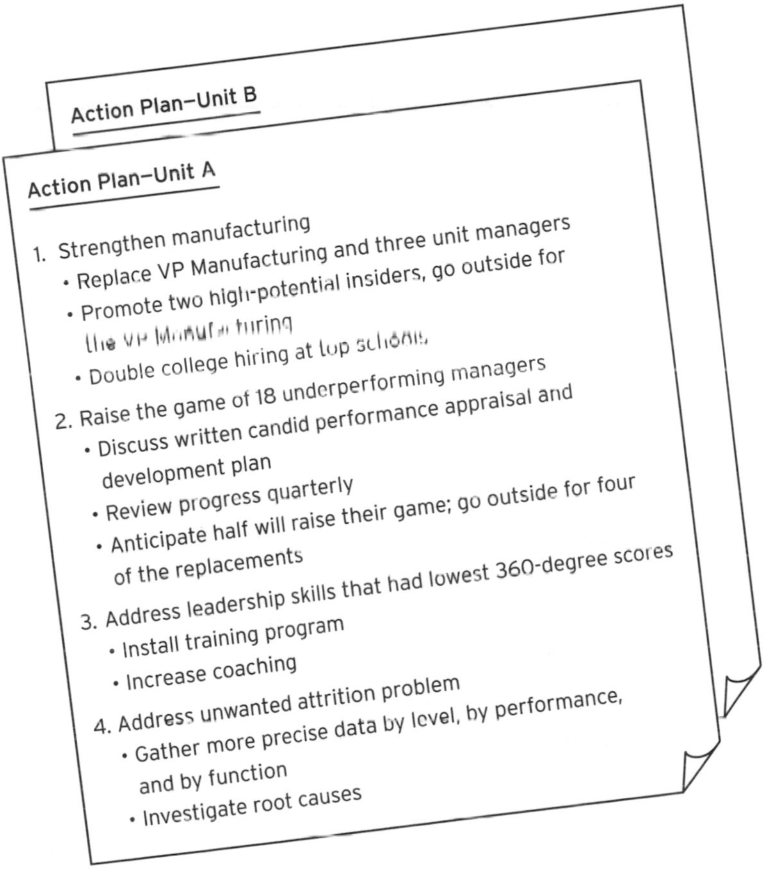

Action Plan—Unit B

Action Plan—Unit A

1. Strengthen manufacturing
   • Replace VP Manufacturing and three unit managers
   • Promote two high-potential insiders, go outside for the VP Manufacturing
   • Double college hiring at top schools

2. Raise the game of 18 underperforming managers
   • Discuss written candid performance appraisal and development plan
   • Review progress quarterly
   • Anticipate half will raise their game; go outside for four of the replacements

3. Address leadership skills that had lowest 360-degree scores
   • Install training program
   • Increase coaching

4. Address unwanted attrition problem
   • Gather more precise data by level, by performance, and by function
   • Investigate root causes

and at the end of each year. The leader's supervisor should do the same. Is the talent pool stronger? Has the leader moved on under-performers? Has unwanted attrition decreased?

Most companies fail to hold their people accountable for building the talent pool. Accountability means that there are consequences for those that deliver on the commitments and those that do not. Accountability requires follow-up.

Conduct formal follow-up meetings on the action plans as part of the company's quarterly operating review. Follow up weekly, inquiring informally into the progress on specific actions. Every phone call, every meeting, every plane ride, and every joint customer call is an opportunity to help and nudge the unit to implement its talent plan.

Who is reviewed, who does the reviewing

At what levels in the organization should the talent reviews be held and how should they be rolled up? Who should participate in the reviews? What role should each participant play? Who should be reviewed? Let us try to answer those questions briefly.

Levels of reviews and roll-up. Each operating unit should conduct a talent review. The exact number for your company will depend on the size of the company, the number of businesses and functional units, and your leaders' capacity to participate in review discussions. If there are multiple units in a division, you will need to conduct a review at the division level that rolls up and consolidates all of the units within that division.

The CEO and senior corporate HR officers should go out to each unit and spend an eight- to twelve-hour day talking about the people in that unit and the overall strength of the talent pool. GE does this for all twenty of its business units, SunTrust for all thirty of its banks, and The Limited for all of its brands and corporate center functions. The review is typically one day per unit, with the CEO chairing the meeting.

Roll up the conclusions from each division to form a perspective for the corporation as a whole. This series of consolidated reviews allows the organization to calibrate assessments across the company.

In small companies, a single talent review process that looks simultaneously at the top 40 to 100 managers is appropriate.

Participants and roles. We mentioned that the CEO and the senior HR officer participate in the review. Their participation is, in fact, essential. The CEO sets the expectations for the review, communicating that candor is required and why. The CEO also pushes the participants to take risks on high-potential individuals, demands decisive action on underperformers, and holds all to a rigorous standard for leadership excellence.

The senior HR executive should push for candor and insight in the discussions. In order to identify development opportunities, he or she should track the inventory of critical jobs and special projects. He or she should also record the assessments and action plans and offer creative solutions for the placement of high-potential managers.

The operating unit's line and HR managers also participate. The managers present the preliminary assessments of their direct reports; use the review as an opportunity to learn about people in the unit outside their line of sight; ask colleagues probing questions that drive to real insight into the strengths, weaknesses, and development needs of people being discussed; push to achieve an expected distribution of ratings for the individuals reviewed; help assess the overall strengths and weaknesses in the unit's talent pool; and own responsibility for all follow-up actions.

People reviewed. When you design your company's review process, go deep into the company so that you are seeing both your current leaders and your future leaders. For example, the review might include the direct reports of the unit's manager and their direct reports, plus ten to twenty up-and-coming leaders from lower levels. By reviewing these future leaders, you will ensure that they are showing up on the radar screen of senior managers earlier than they might otherwise have. A large company's review might cover the top 400 to 800 managers across the company. A smaller company might focus only on its top 40 to 100 managers.

Getting started

The review process doesn't need to be perfect in order to get started. The best performing companies, in fact, tend to have a talent review process that is light on formality and heavy on intensity. They are focused on the importance of talent. They recognize that their processes and assessment skills will improve as they go along. Consider the case of National Australia Bank.[17]

When Frank Cicutto became CEO in 1999, he installed a new, more rigorous talent review process in which he, his six direct reports, and his senior HR officer independently evaluated the top 100 officers of the company. They then compared their separate evaluations and debated the points of difference until they had reached a joint assessment. Because they had never had a rigorous review or differentiation process before this, Cicutto stipulated that 25 percent of the people being reviewed would be named top performers and 25 percent bottom performers. In the process of defining these top and bottom players, Cicutto and his colleagues began, for the first time, to crystallize their definition of leadership at the bank.

Translating the assessments into actions called for some courage— and some actions that went against the paternalistic corporate culture. Initially, the proposed actions were rather "soft"—the A players got a slight bump in compensation, for example, and the C players were singled out for special training.

Cicutto, however, soon realized that these actions were not enough to signal that the company was moving to a meritocracy, where the consequences of great and poor performance would be quite different. So he insisted they take another pass at the As and the Cs, this time with more "hard" actions. Significant promotions, large salary increases, and high-profile special assignments were the kind of hard actions for the As. Compensation freezes and "managing out" were the hard actions for the Cs. In the first pass, hard actions had been preliminarily agreed to on only 20 percent of the As and Cs. However, after the second pass, hard actions were agreed to on 70 percent of the As and the Cs. This led to important early changes in the top 100 and sent a visible signal throughout the company that performance counted and that management was very serious about strengthening the talent pool.

One of the things that made the talent review process successful was the fact that Cicutto and his top team "nailed their flag to the mast" in regard to their own personal commitment. They made sure that leadership development and personal coaching began with themselves. At a recent senior management conference, Cicutto observed the impact that the talent review process has had on the company. Only four of the sixty top executives were in the same position at the time of the meeting as they were when Cicutto took over as CEO.

The New Start

By investing in your A players, affirming and growing your Bs, and acting on your Cs, you can raise your company's performance to levels that today might be hard to imagine. To get started, you could begin with a quick and efficient talent review process, as did National Australia Bank and The Limited. You could meet with each business unit head separately to agree on the five to seven actions they should take to substantially strengthen their talent pools. You could tie 30 percent of their compensation to the execution of those initiatives. Furthermore, you could immediately start to model the affirming behaviors you want your colleagues to emulate.

Remember, it's not the formality of the talent review process that matters; it's the quality of the dialogue, the clarity and boldness of the action plans, and the follow-through that will drive your company's performance higher. Differentiating and affirming your people will make your organization the meritocracy your talented managers want it to be.

7

GET STARTED–
AND EXPECT HUGE
IMPACT IN A YEAR

In this last chapter, we will help you think about how to get started on the journey toward a stronger talent pool. Should you start by strengthening the EVP? By moving your top performers and underperformers into new jobs? By revitalizing your recruiting program?

Regardless of where you start, we will try to convince you that you should expect huge impact in the first year. If you don't, you aren't thinking about your talent opportunity boldly enough. If you start too cautiously or incrementally, your efforts will fizzle out, and so will your resolve.

Winning the war for talent will take a conscious, sustained effort. What you do in the first year is just the beginning of a long journey. Building a strong talent pool will require a fundamentally new approach to the way you think about and manage talent. Indeed it will require a fundamental shift in the way you run your business and carry out your leadership responsibilities. But there is promise and excitement in that challenge that we hope you will find invigorating.

A Crossroad That Is Easy to Miss

At the beginning of this book, we talked about Andy Grove's strategic inflection points, and we asserted that the decision to make talent a top corporate priority is one such strategic inflection point. It is one that is surprisingly easy to underestimate—or miss entirely.

Despite all the rhetoric about the talent wars, most companies are indeed missing this critical crossroad. Yes, the leaders of these companies have noticed that the winds have shifted. Yes, they now recognize that finding the people they need is harder than ever. But only 26 percent of the 6,900 managers we surveyed in our recent research strongly agreed that talent is a top priority at their companies.[1]

Many companies don't know where they stand in the war for talent. They aren't measuring their share of the talent market against that of their competitors. They don't track attrition in any insightful, actionable way. No one brings the CEO the bad news about losses of high performers down the line, lack of candor in the culture, the disproportionate share of low performers, or weak recruiting results. Furthermore, the board is not asking the CEO or senior management about the strength of the talent pool. The black-and-white contrast between the old and new talent mindsets are, for most companies, shades of gray.

It's easy to underestimate the war for talent. It is tempting to say that you have enough talent and could not find better if you tried, that the departure of young high performers is understandable, and that not bringing A+ leaders into the top of the organization is wise. It is tempting to make incremental changes (more stock options, beefing up HR, a leadership training program, etc.) and declare that you are doing all you can. It is tempting to assume that during a softer economy you don't have to worry about the war for talent.

Let's be clear: Making real changes will be difficult and will require zeal, fortitude, and courage. It must have been difficult for Arthur Blank of The Home Depot to bring in six top-level senior executives, kick himself upstairs, and ultimately retire at fifty-eight.

Or for Phil Humann at SunTrust Banks to invest $50 million to get more and better people. It must have been difficult for Greg Summe to replace nine of his ten direct reports within a year at PerkinElmer. It must have been difficult for Jeff Skilling to say that people should flow freely to new units at Enron even though they might leave gaping holes in the units they left.

Is Talent a Priority?

To get started, you must ask yourself if you will commit to making talent a strategic priority. We encourage you to think about your company's competitive advantage and the role better talent will play in driving its success. Do you have the talent pool you need to meet your aspirations? Will strengthening your talent pool improve your company's success over the next few years? We encourage you to debate this with your colleagues, particularly with your middle managers, who may see signs of problems even sooner than your senior executives.

Take some measurements. What is the attrition rate of your best midlevel managers? How many open positions do you have now versus two years ago? What percentage of your top 50 or 500 managers have the potential to be promoted two levels and what percentage are already over their heads? How much more productive are your top performers than your average performers?

Then make a conscious choice: Should strengthening your talent pool be a top three priority? Are you prepared to make talent management a much bigger part of your job? Are you willing to take bold actions to strengthen your talent pool? Make this decision with your team.

In the great majority of cases we think you will decide, "Yes, talent must be a top priority for us." But don't reach that conclusion if you aren't truly prepared to embark on significant change. There's no point in making small incremental changes. Forcing yourself and your team to make an explicit decision is the first step.

Decide Where to Start

Once you have established talent as one of your top three priorities, you have to decide where to start. You can't tackle everything at once, and you can't go from poor practice to world-class practice overnight. You have to figure out which changes will have the most impact—and make those happen in a big way.

Over the last four years, we have discussed the talent challenge with more than 200 companies. We have observed three situations that typically spur a company to get serious about talent: When they need to dramatically improve their performance; when they have a hiring or retention crisis; and when they recognize that their basic talent management disciplines are woefully inadequate. Admittedly, these situations overlap somewhat, but we were able to place almost all of our twenty-seven case companies in one of the three situations. Each of these situations has its own urgency and each has its own priorities. Your company's situation will be somewhat unique, but reading about what companies in these situations did will give you ideas about how to get started on a path to a stronger talent pool.

Situation 1: Dramatic performance or growth improvement

When companies aspire to achieve a dramatic performance improvement—be that a turnaround, a much steeper growth curve, or new types of businesses—they often need to substantially strengthen their talent pool. When leaders are in this situation, it is critical that they face this challenge squarely. They must take sufficiently bold action to dramatically strengthen the talent pool. The Home Depot, for example, strengthened its executive talent pool because it wanted to pursue six new growth areas. SunTrust needed more and better people to increase its growth rate from 4 percent to 10 percent. Greg Summe needed better talent when he became CEO of an underperforming company. Les Wexner at The Limited found the talent religion because his management approach wasn't working anymore and performance had declined.

Companies in this situation have to simultaneously boost the performance drivers of the business *and* build a stronger talent pool. The direct actions to boost business performance might include portfolio restructuring; better financial performance and measurement systems; crucial initiatives to boost quality, productivity, or purchasing effectiveness (as Summe did at PerkinElmer); and launching new products or going into new business areas (as The Home Depot did).

You will certainly have to raise the performance expectations of every unit and perhaps change your incentive plans, but you must also dramatically strengthen the talent pool. To do so, you will need to inject a lot of new talent into the organization. You may need to replace a substantial number of people who are simply not up to the challenge. You will also need to quickly develop your high-potential people to their full potential.

Performance and talent-building feed on each other's success: Exciting business challenges attract high-caliber people, and high-caliber people help address those challenges. Don't blink on the talent issues. Don't assume the same old team will magically learn new tricks. Don't think special projects or new processes alone will be enough to substantially change the performance trajectory of the company—they won't. You will have to face up to the talent issues, and as a leader you must invest as much energy in strengthening the talent pool as you do in driving the performance and restructuring initiatives. Better talent and better performance are inextricably linked.

To strengthen the talent pool, start by taking inventory of the talent in the positions that are critical to the performance improvement. What are the skills required to achieve the new aspirations? What percentage of the incumbents in key positions will be able to deliver on the new level of performance? Do you have enough people to drive the new growth plans? Who are the strong people you can leverage and who are the people who will hold you back? When SunTrust inventoried its talent, 10 percent of the 200 line-of-business managers were underleveraged and 20 percent were in over their heads. When Greg Summe did this as he took over the reins at PerkinElmer, he found 80 of the top 100 managers needed to be replaced. Half of the replacements came from the inside, and the other half came from the outside.

When requiring a dramatic performance improvement, you don't need an elaborate process for assessing your talent. It only has to be good enough to quickly get a read on who will be able to deliver at the new performance levels and who will not. Collect the existing information on each person (intrinsic skills, past performance and accomplishments, etc.), get evaluative input from the three or four people who have the best perspective on each person, and then get the leadership team together to discuss each person. Use some simple, helpful tools such as the ones described in chapter 6. Repeat the talent review process every six months, refining the assessments and continuously adjusting your action plans.

Next, take action. Recruit outsiders who can set a new performance standard and bring new skills and perspectives. Identify the people in the organization who are not up to the challenge and move them out—if not out of the company, then out of the critical positions. Give your A players more responsibility and move them into the most critical positions. Promote a few superstars from two or three levels down in the organization.

Start by getting your top ten people right, then work closely with them to get the next 100 to 200 right. If you don't get your immediate reports right you will give up huge leverage and credibility. Push the talent upgrade process down through the organization within the first twelve to eighteen months.

Situation 2: A hiring or retention crisis

Some companies face a crisis situation when recruiting suddenly fails, or when they start losing talent to other more attractive options. In this situation, a dramatic strengthening of the EVP is needed.

SunTrust's Mimi Breeden faced a crisis in attrition and had to look hard at her EVP, as did many consulting firms and investment banks when they suddenly lost people to start-ups and venture capital firms in the late 1990s. As the war for talent persists, the need to strengthen EVPs will come into sharper focus.

Start by determining why high performers are leaving and why recruits are turning down offers. Breeden conducted exit interviews to pinpoint why her people were leaving. Likewise, you must analyze who is leaving, where they are going, and which groups within your company are losing the most people. Investigate which aspects of your EVP are attracting people and which are pushing them away. Think of the attrition or recruiting problem as you would a marketing problem. Conduct a rigorous analysis of what potential recruits want. Assess your competitor's EVP and determine how yours stacks up against theirs.

Decide which aspects of your EVP you want to strengthen. Level 3 Communications decided to locate itself in Colorado. Synovus Financial built a strong, people-focused culture. Go beyond the routine perks to the things that make a real difference to your target people. Be prepared to change the way you do business and move out of your comfort zone, as Breeden did.

Situation 3: Inadequate talent management disciplines

Some companies get the talent religion when they realize that their talent disciplines are inadequate. They may have good people, good performance, and good growth prospects. They may know intuitively that talent will be a key driver of success in their future. But their talent processes are weak or nonexistent. Often these are companies that were very successful in one business but now they want to enter new arenas. Sometimes they are midsize companies on the cusp of becoming something much larger. These companies typically do not have a rigorous talent review process or a real recruiting strategy. There is no institutionalized development through coaching or deliberate job moves. There is no process to make sure the high performers are kept engaged and excited.

For companies in this situation, there are four steps to take at the start. First, link talent to strategy and identify the gaps. Enron, for instance, dramatically strengthened its entry-level recruiting. Amgen identified various functional gaps. Second, put more emphasis on development. Amgen, for instance, already had many great people, but needed to explicitly develop them. CEO Kevin Sharer identi-fied twenty potential stars and gave them a series of development moves. The Home Depot started using 360-degree feedback to ensure that every manager understood his or her strengths and weaknesses.

Third, put in place some simple, robust talent management processes. Enron, Amgen, and The Home Depot all now have a tal-ent review process. They all have candid, written performance reviews. All three use 360-degree feedback and all three are com-mitted to leadership training. As Sharer said, "There is huge lever-age in acing Talent Management 101."

Fourth, companies in this situation should develop a strong HR function. The Home Depot, Amgen, and Enron all have strength-ened their HR function throughout their organizations, so that each division has a strong HR generalist, rather than technicians. Line and staff managers must drive the talent management process, of course, but a highly effective HR organization is helpful.

Companies that have effortlessly attracted a good talent pool—perhaps because they are hot young players in a hot industry—have a tendency to look at HR functions and talent processes as exercises with little value. But other hot companies such as Enron, Amgen, and The Home Depot, for instance, recognize them as prerequisites for an even bigger future.

To get started on your talent-building effort, ask yourself the questions in the box. If you have ten to twelve "yes" answers, you are a benchmark company. We applaud you and encourage you to keep driving your efforts hard. If you have seven to nine "yes" answers, you have made talent a priority and are well on the jour-ney. Work hard on the several areas where you have "no" answers. If you answer "yes" to six or fewer of the above questions, the good news is you have a lot of company. We believe (based on our expe-rience with more than 200 companies) that the average score for most companies is around three to four "yes" answers. The bad news is you have a long way to go and your competitors may have, or soon may get, the jump on you.

ARE YOU PREPARED TO WIN THE WAR FOR TALENT?

1. Is talent one of your top three priorities?
2. Are you spending 30 percent or more of your time strengthening your talent pool? Have you made talent your job?
3. Are you and all your key people explicitly held accountable for strengthening their talent pool?
4. Do you have a winning EVP that attracts talented people to your organization?
5. Do you know the attrition rate of your young high-performing managers and why they are leaving? Do you have initiatives in place to reduce these regretted losses?
6. Are you aggressively recruiting for new faces in new places at all levels, including senior levels, of your organization?
7. Does your unit have a robust written recruiting strategy, similar in rigor to your marketing strategies?
8. Do you give your top performers accelerated development opportunities, significantly differentiated compensation, and real mentoring?
9. Does your organization have a culture of candid feedback and helpful coaching?
10. Does your organization have a talent review process that has the importance and intensity of the budget process and that cascades throughout your organization?
11. Is the review session filled with candor and does it result in real consequences for those discussed?
12. Is your annual forced attrition rate in the 5 to 10 percent range, and are you continuously dealing with underperformers?

Expect Huge Impact in the First Year

Although the talent journey will be continuous, you should expect impact from your efforts within the first year. If you don't, you are not being sufficiently aggressive. You are not investing enough time and money in strengthening your talent pool. You are not setting the talent bar high enough. Expect huge impact in the first year and craft a program that will achieve that.

This was a complete surprise to us. We expected to find that the talent payoff would be uncertain in terms of time and extent, often requiring three, four, or even five years before producing any real impact. Our thinking has changed. We now realize that impact in a year is the rule rather than the exception. Remember, SunTrust increased its growth rate from 4 percent to 10 percent in one year, primarily through more and better people. PerkinElmer tripled its market value in less than two years by strengthening its management ranks while restructuring the business. Mimi Breeden reduced her unit's turnover of high performers by 80 percent in eighteen months by making talent her job and the job of her direct reports. Larry Bossidy created a culture of candor in less than a year at AlliedSignal by giving his direct reports written, balanced, candid feedback.

What typifies each of these situations is that the leaders made an aggressive commitment to achieve substantial impact quickly. It was not some optional deal. Better talent and better performance were top priorities for all leaders up and down the line. By contrast, we often see incremental changes, caution, and lots of talk. Many other companies would have been much more cautious than SunTrust and invested perhaps $5 million, rather than the $50 million that SunTrust did. Many leaders would have exhorted candor, whereas Bossidy operationalized it by personally writing two-page memos to each of his direct reports containing candid, constructive feedback.

Chuck Okosky, formerly Vice President of Executive Development at GE, takes the idea of immediate impact a step farther. "By placing A players in key jobs, you should expect impact right away—not a year later," he says. "When Larry Johnson became the head of GE's Medical Systems business in Europe in June 1996," Okosky continues, "one of his first steps was to assemble his full European officer team in the Prague sales office. In his opening remarks, Johnson told them he expected a substantial increase in sales and described in detail how that could be accomplished. "Next, they visited customers for six hours (which most of the headquarters' staff had not done in months), asking 'How can we earn more of your business?' They met that evening to draw up action plans for each account, which were executed immediately. In one day the aspirations and can-do attitude of the team began to change, and improved results began to arrive in just a matter of months."

The war for talent requires this kind of urgency. The old mind-set was, "Investing in talent is a good thing to do, but the payout is uncertain, so let's be cautious. Let's not overinvest. Let's go slow. Let's try an initiative or two. Let's get HR to do it." The new mind-set is, "We should expect substantial, measurable results in a year if we, as leaders up and down the line, each make a commitment to strengthening our talent pool, and commit to all the actions necessary to do that."

Remember, It's an Endless Journey

You can achieve huge impact in a year, but talent building isn't a program that begins and ends. Rather, it is a continuous and fundamentally new way of managing the business. Talent management has to become embedded in the leaders' concept of their jobs. Reviewing and constantly strengthening the talent pool have to become as central to running the business as planning, new products, productivity improvement, and budgeting.

There will always be a next talent-building priority for every company. The model companies that we look to for inspiration and best practices are themselves striving for the next level of sophistication in how they manage talent.

"Talent has been my number one priority for three years; it is my number one priority now; and it will be my number one priority three years from now," as Greg Summe said earlier. Even though Summe has dramatically strengthened his top 200 managers, instilled a talent mindset in his sector heads and many others, and tripled his company's market cap, he is striving for even more. Summe gives the company poor marks on pushing the talent review process beyond the top 200. He feels they are not developing enough global managers. And he knows they have more to do to create an open and trusting environment. Summe has higher ambitions for PerkinElmer and sees ever-increasing opportunity to create substantial shareholder value. He believes the company can achieve this only by building the best talent in every business, in every function, and in every geography. And he admits, "We have a long way to go to accomplish that."

Although Amgen has a strong talent mindset and a powerful EVP, it, too, recognizes it has only begun. Yes, the team at the top has a "talent is my job" midset. Their EVP is world class. They are committed to development. In truth, however, Amgen is only now putting a robust talent review process in place. Candor is still a struggle. Amgen also admits that its talent pipeline still needs much improvement before the company can claim to be one of the world's great therapeutics companies, competing successfully against Merck and Pfizer.

The same could be said for SunTrust. It has boosted its growth rate almost threefold in one year through its talent management initiatives, but it has more to do. In fact, in agreeing to participate in the research for this book, CEO Phil Humann insisted that we not overplay the bank's progress over the past three years. "We are maybe halfway there," he admitted. Humann explained that Sun-Trust has made improvements in strengthening the quality of its talent, hiring external people, developing a talent management process, and moving on low performers, but the company is nowhere near finished. The bar keeps rising. Growth has slowed, competition has heated up, and margins are down. "Not only do we have new ground to cover, but we also have to make sure that we maintain what we've already accomplished," says Humann. "We have to continue to deepen our talent pools, deliver better development opportunities to our people, and focus on retention of our younger people. Yes, the bar keeps going up. I bet we still have 20 percent underperformers against the new bar. I know we have to focus on exciting our younger people—not to mention that we have to add speed to the equation."

Think of it this way: GE has been working on talent harder, longer, and better than any company we have observed, and they have been doing it for more than forty years. Yet GE still goes outside for about 20 percent of its top 500 openings. It still aggressively acts on the least effective managers at every level of the organization every year. And, until he stepped down, Jack Welch continued to spend 50 percent of his time on talent issues. Companies already very good at talent management, like GE, are constantly improving the way they manage talent. Every company has to keep innovating just to keep up.

Yes, that sounds like a never-ending trek! The good news is this: You can expect results in less than one year. Georgia-Pacific is an encouraging case in point.

Georgia-Pacific Packaging

Georgia-Pacific Packaging produces a lot of corrugated boxes; in fact, their 1997 revenues from corrugated boxes were approximately $1.4 billion. These boxes are made at fifty packaging facilities around the United States. To an outsider, making corrugated boxes may seem like a simple business with little room for innovation or performance improvement. It turns out, however, that making corrugated boxes and running a packaging facility is a highly technical task requiring deep industry-specific skills and committed leadership.

Early in 1998, Steve Macadam became the new Senior Vice President of Georgia-Pacific's Containerboard & Packaging Division. In the first three months, Macadam went to work with his team of five regional managers on a range of performance improvement issues, from productivity to safety to quality. It quickly became clear that improvement in all areas was contingent on the strength of the packaging facility general managers (GMs).

Macadam, now the Executive Vice President of Pulp & Paperboard, began by asking the five regional managers to come together to assess the fifty GMs. "Steve insisted on candor," one of the regional managers recalled. "We had hard conversations about each individual, lasting hours at a time." Macadam required each of the regional managers to write a one-page evaluation of each GM.

On a five-point scale, the regional managers had to rank each GM on strategic thinking, leadership, performance ethic, and financial results.

"Steve worked closely with us," recalled one manager. "He visited all fifty managers and he listened. He pushed. He was willing to accept disagreement." Together, the group established five principles of effective talent management: candor, differentiation, consequence management, caring about people and their careers, and affirmation.

As a result of this assessment, the regional managers and Macadam decided to replace almost half of the GMs. "There was just no way that some of these people had a place in our organization," Macadam recalls, "yet making these changes was still a difficult thing to do." He especially struggled with the terminations. "You don't sleep because you know these people have families and will have to go home and tell their kids that they lost their jobs." In Macadam's first twenty months, twenty-two GMs were moved through a combination of early retirements, lateral and corrective moves, terminations, and some resignations.

Finding new managers entailed intense recruiting, but within six months, the new GMs were hired. Six came from the ranks of Georgia-Pacific, and the rest were hired from the outside with proven track records in the industry. The regional managers and Macadam went to work with each of the fifty packaging facilities to establish goals in productivity, quality, safety, and profits. Even with the new and improved GMs in place, it wasn't easy.

As they progressed with their plans, they began to realize that replacing the GMs was not going to change their business overnight. Talent deficiencies existing deep within each packaging facility would have to be addressed before real change could take place. The problem was that many of the facilities had been run the same way by the same people for the last twenty-five years. There was a strong resistance to change.

At the packaging facility in Chicago, for instance, the new manager, Steve Wells, found that extreme measures were required.

"When I took over as the GM in February 1999, the plant had not made a profit in over twenty years. In fact, the plant had lost $5.3 million in 1998. Safety incidents were at an all-time high and the plant was just recovering from the shock of a near fatality. We're located in a high-risk security area on the south side of town and personal safety outside the facility has always been an issue. Overall, it was not a happy place."

With guidance from his regional manager, Wells first attacked the talent issue. He interviewed and evaluated all the key players (salaried and then hourly). Wells found that for the most part he had a hard-working group of individuals who simply lacked direction, incentive, and leadership. "Once I shared with all 130 employees at the plant the real meaning behind our losses and opened their eyes to why we had to turn things around, I immediately saw a difference. These guys hadn't had anyone care about them or their careers in years. Those who didn't buy into my change philosophy . . . well, they self-selected out."

Indeed, ten of Wells's twenty-six salaried employees left in the first six months.

Once Wells had his team in place he worked hard on connecting with his people. He instituted a Monday morning meeting in which each of the salaried employees reported on his or her department. Wells now gets these individuals to fine-tune the mission and goals of the plant once a month through team-building exercises that force them to voice problems without throwing stones. From these discussions, task forces are formed and held responsible for resolution. Adds Wells, "Now we're people-focused and performance-driven. It's been amazing to watch people grow and respond positively over the last year."

Wells's results were gratifying: Within one year the facility's employees were functioning as a team again. Accidents declined from seven to two, and annual profits rose from a loss of $0.4 million in 1999 to a profit of $3.3 million in 2000. For all of his success and hard work as a talent manager, Wells was recently awarded the Coin of Excellence in Leadership by Georgia-Pacific. Reflecting on the

MOST BOARDS OF DIRECTORS NEGLECT THE TALENT LEVER

Another group of leaders who should be playing a significant role in ensuring that the company has a strong talent pool—but isn't—is the board of directors. Are they guilty, then, of neglect?

Boards have not traditionally been responsible for the talent vitality of their companies. When we recently studied the annual reports of fifty major U.S. companies, in fact, not a single one had a talent committee. This exclusion represents a missed opportunity.

Most boards help choose new CEOs, of course, and the compensation committees decide on compensation for the top five to twenty officers. However, our survey of 400 corporate officers across thirty-five companies indicated that beyond those roles, the board of directors does not play a significant role in helping strengthen the talent pool of the company. In fact, when asked, only 26 percent of corporate officers somewhat or strongly agreed that the board of directors really knows the strengths and weaknesses of their company's top 20 to 100 executives.[2]

How can directors make intelligent compensation decisions without understanding the strengths and weaknesses of the officers? When asked the question, "Does the board probe for organizational strengths and weaknesses of each division?" only 27 percent strongly or somewhat agreed. When asked if the board plays an important role in strengthening the overall talent pool of the company, only 35 percent agreed.[3]

What happens all too frequently is that the CEO profiles the top ten to twenty-five officers of the company for the board—an annual exercise that might take a few hours. There are some polite questions, perhaps even one or two probing questions about an officer who is struggling, or some quick suggestions regarding an open position, and then it's on to cocktails. Perhaps this is an overstatement, but not as much as you might think.

award, Wells said, "Even when we thought this plant was going to be sold six months ago, I decided to stay. I would rather stay with these guys than be transferred to another plant within GP. I wouldn't trade the team I've built and how far we've come together for anything."

Terry Cinotte, one of the five regional managers, was struck by the changes the new GMs, like Wells, were capable of making. He

Imagine how much more the board could do. Most corporate boards have between 200 and 400 years of collective experience, much of it in the industries the company participates in. Many experienced directors know (or should know) what gold-standard talent looks like and where to find it. Typically, though, they do not share that with the company.

Here is what we suggest boards do:

1. Form a talent committee of the board. Staff it with the three or four directors who have the best talent mindset.

2. Ensure that the CEO, COO, and senior division leaders of the company have a talent mindset as outlined earlier.

3. Ensure that the corporation's talent review process is rigorous and probing, and that it produces action-packed, measurable plans to develop the strength of the talent pool in each division throughout the company.

4. Hold an annual two-day retreat in which the CEO and executive vice president of HR report on the strength of the company's talent pool.

5. Provide ongoing and proactive advice to the CEO and key leaders of the company on strengthening their talent pools.

We recently asked Mike Ruettgers, Executive Chairman of EMC, what he learned from serving on PerkinElmer's board. He said, "Greg Summe updates the board at every meeting on the outcomes of the talent review process and his talent initiatives. Most companies don't do this. Hence, most boards don't focus on the strength and development of the talent pool of a company in any systematic, ongoing way." He added, "I'd encourage any company I am a director of to have such a process. It has fundamentally changed my view of how to run a business. Needless to say, we have started incorporating such a process at EMC, and I welcome my board's help."[4]

notes, "I then understood what Macadam meant about talent. I used to spend 70 percent of my time driving initiatives and directing people. With my new GMs, however, I didn't have to drive or direct." It was a lesson that changed his mind about talent. "Now I spend 70 percent of my time getting talented leaders in key slots in my facilities. I know now that talent is the key."

What convinced Cinotte was the financial benefit that came with good talent management. "Give me a brand new facility with an average leader and the facility will make $1 million a year," he says. "Compare that to an old facility with talented leadership, and it will make $3 million to $4 million a year. I'll pay the average manager a $115,000 salary and a $60,000 bonus. But I'll pay the exceptional manager a $135,000 salary and a $90,000 bonus. So for $50,000 more, I get an incremental $2 million to $3 million per year in profit."

So why didn't he realize this before? "We had no talent review system, no candor, no consequence management. We spent no time on the talent topic and, frankly, we didn't realize better talent would make such a huge difference," concludes Cinotte.

When the smoke cleared after the first full year, Macadam and his five regional managers had changed 96 of the top 246 people. With the new team in place, Macadam and his team had increased profits from $20 million to $80 million in one year without price increases in the industry.

With the massive talent upgrade behind him, Macadam is now turning his attention to the longer term. Georgia-Pacific has started to build a strong education program for managers, benchmarked on the renowned training programs at furniture maker Milliken. "We believe our people want to be developed, can be developed, and want to do a good job," he says. "They'll receive ongoing education—evidence of the company's commitment to them." Macadam describes Georgia-Pacific's four principles for effective education. Number one, always put the most qualified person in the job, not just those who have been trained for it. Number two, people must raise their hand to go to training; they've got to want it. Number three, the training must be timely. Number four, you've got to find a way to measure the impact of the training.

Says Macadam, "We say to our people, 'If you want to be a facility manager there are four technical skills and three leadership skills that you need and here's how you currently stack up on each. Fully aware of where you stand, it's now up to you. I recommend that

you get some coaching and feedback, and consider signing yourself up for an education program. Yes, results count a lot but you've
got to have the skills to perform at the next level before we'll promote you.'"

Profits up from $20 million to $80 million in one year, a meritocracy in place, people more excited and energized about their
work, and a benchmarked education program launched. That
sounds like pretty good impact for one year.

The McCallie School

All the case stories presented so far in this book have been about
businesses. But to demonstrate the impact that improving the talent pool can have on the performance of any organization—be it a
government agency, orchestra, church, synagogue, or even a boys'
school set in the hills of Tennessee—we offer this final story.

The McCallie School has been a successful preparatory school
for boys for more than ninety years. Located just below Mission-
ary Ridge in Chattanooga, Tennessee, the school educates 880 boys
in grades six through twelve. The school was always one of the best
in terms of values, core curriculum, and esprit de corps. However,
in terms of standardized test scores and college placements, McCallie was perhaps half a step behind the great Eastern boarding
schools. The top boys have always been exceptional in academics
and leadership, but there weren't enough of them.

To strengthen the program, McCallie and a few alumni established an Honors Scholar program to attract top ninth- and tenth-
grade boarding students. Patterned on the world-renowned
Morehead merit scholarship program at the University of North
Carolina, the McCallie scholarship would be based on tough criteria: To win the scholarship, students would have to have standardized test scores in the top 10 percent nationwide and excellent
grades. They would also have to show outstanding character and
leadership potential.

McCallie established committees of alumni to recruit throughout
the eastern and southern parts of the country. They asked counselors

at good public schools and other preparatory schools to spread the word. The school's board of directors raised $12 million to endow as many as seventeen scholarships each year. In the first year, sixty boys were nominated. Two received full scholarships, ten were offered half scholarships, and thirteen were offered one-quarter scholarships. Seventeen accepted and matriculated into McCallie's class of 2000.

The impact of this talent infusion was immediate. The new recruits were instant leaders in the dorms, on the athletic fields, and in the student council. The ninth-grade standardized test scores jumped from 47 percent to 67 percent. Not only did they raise the standards at the school, they also inspired most of the other students to achieve more than ever before. Because these new students required less attention, teachers had more time to spend with struggling students. "The enthusiasm of the honor students and the level of dedication and leadership they bring is infectious," says Upper School Head Kenny Sholl. "That kind of excitement rubs off on the other students. Suddenly it's cool to be involved in activities and to do well academically."

Says Jacob, a senior from South Carolina, "Because of the opportunities I've been given at McCallie, I know I will do something meaningful with my future. And I know I need to give back to this community while I'm here. I try to lead by example, encouraging other students to get involved in school activities and helping them with their homework. I try to be a friend to everyone. What I get in return are an amazing group of friends and an opportunity to stretch academically."

Headmaster Kirk Walker is justifiably proud. "In one year we dramatically improved the ninth grade," he explains. "In three years we'll improve the entire character of the school—in the dorms, on the athletic fields, as well as in the classrooms." He adds, "Bringing in exceptional talent challenges the other boys, the teachers, the administrators, the curriculum, and the institution in general to be better. The rising tide of talent is lifting all boats."

The Talent Tide

The rising tide of talent is lifting all boats. It's a statement that applies to a boys' school in Tennessee. But it also applies to Enron, Amgen, PerkinElmer, SunTrust, The Limited, Arrow Electronics, and many other companies. It could also apply to your organization—and to you—if you expect uncommonly great things from your talent efforts.

Whether you are just getting started or are already actively engaged in your company's talent management improvements, we urge you to act boldly and to persevere. Remember, talent is an endless journey, not a destination. As Symantec CEO John Thompson wryly noted, "Sometimes I think that fighting the talent war is like racing up Heartbreak Hill in the Boston Marathon. But really, it's more like a ceaseless sprint on a treadmill. A race has an ending point, but this thing just keeps on running!"

We hope the principles you have learned in this book and the practitioners you have met will imbue you with courage, energy, and inspiration. You *can* have immediate and substantial impact on your organization's performance—if you believe passionately in your talent agenda, understand the hopes and aspirations of your people, stretch them, encourage them, give them your time and attention, and infuse candor and caring into all your people efforts. In the process, the talents entrusted to you (including your own) will multiply, as they did in the biblical parable, and your organization will indeed prosper.

APPENDIX

THE WAR FOR
TALENT SURVEYS

I n the About the War for Talent Research section we explained the
objectives and participants in McKinsey & Company's War for
Talent Surveys. In this appendix we add a few additional points of
detail about the survey methodology.

Participating Companies

In 1997, seventy-seven large U.S. based companies participated in
the War for Talent Survey (see figure A-1). Three types of questionnaires were sent to these companies for three different respondent
groups: corporate officers, senior managers, and the most senior
HR executive. Companies could choose to participate in one, two,
or all three of the surveys. Forty companies participated in the corporate officer survey, fifty companies participated in the senior
managers survey, and seventy-two companies participated in the
HR executive survey.

In 2000, thirty-five large U.S.-based companies and nineteen
midsized U.S.-based companies participated in the War for Talent
Survey (see figure A-2). Three types of questionnaires were sent to

Figure A-1 Seventy-Seven Large Companies Participated in 1997

Abbott Labs	Delta Air Lines	Nationwide
ADP	Eckerd	Nucor
Alcan Aluminium	El Paso Energy	PacifiCare Health Systems
Alcoa	Electronic Data Systems	Philip Morris
AlliedSignal	EMC	ReliaStar Financial
American Electric Power	Enron	ReSound
Ameritech	General Electric	Reynolds & Reynolds
Amgen	Harley-Davidson	Sears, Roebuck and Co.
Arrow Electronics	Hewlett-Packard	Service Merchandise
Baan	Intel	Sherwin Williams
BancOne/First USA	International Paper	St. Paul Companies
Baxter International	Intuit	Staples
Becton Dickinson	Johnson & Johnson	SunTrust Banks
BellSouth	KeyCorp	Tech Data
Best Foods	KP Health Plan	Terra Industries
Bristol-Myers Squibb	& Hospitals of CA	Texaco
Burlington Northern	May Department Stores	Textron
& Santa Fe Railroad	McKinsey & Company	The Gap
Campbell Soup Company	Mead	The Home Depot
Cardinal Health	Medtronic	Transamerica
Chase Manhattan	Merck & Co.	U.S. West
Chevron	Monsanto Company	United Technologies
Chicago Title & Trust	Nabisco	Viacom
CIGNA Healthcare	Nacco Industries	Virginia Power
CINergy	National Service	Wells Fargo
Clorox	Industries	Williams Companies
CVS	NationsBank	

three respondent groups: corporate officers, senior managers, and mid-managers. All companies participated in all three surveys.

Definition of High- and Average-Performing Companies

In the War for Talent 1997 Survey, we defined high-performing and average-performing companies by their ten-year total return to shareholders. We sorted the list of publicly traded companies based in the United States using their two-digit Standard Industry Code

Figure A-2 Thirty-Five Large Companies Participated in 2000

ADP	Cox Communications	National Service Industries
Alcoa	Edison International	Owens Corning
American Express	First USA Bank	PPG Industries
Arrow Electronics	GATX Corp	PerkinElmer
Avery Dennison	Hughes Electronics	Rockwell International
Baxter International	Huntington Bankshares	SLM Holding Corp.
Belk Stores Services	J.P. Morgan & Co.	SunTrust Banks
Bristol-Myers Squibb	Lincoln Financial	The Hartford
Campbell Soup Company	Merrill Lynch	The Limited Inc.
Cargill	Micro-Warehouse	Wells Fargo
CINergy	Morgan Stanley Dean Witter	Young & Rubicam
CNF Transportation	National City Corp.	

(SIC) and then ranked the companies in each SIC group according to ten-year total return to shareholder (TRS) data. We deemed those companies that placed in the top quintile of TRS to be high-performing. We deemed those that placed in the middle quintile average-performing. We invited companies only in the top and middle quintiles to participate. Forty-four of the participating companies were considered high-performing and thirty-three were considered average.

In the War for Talent 2000 Survey, the large companies were defined as high- or average-performing using the same methodology of ranking companies in each SIC group. This time, however, three- or five-year TRS data were used, rather than ten-year. Of the thirty-five large companies, we deemed eleven high-performing and eight average-performing.

NOTES

Chapter 1

1. Andrew S. Grove, *Only the Paranoid Survive* (New York: Currency Doubleday, 1999), chapter 4.
2. Kenneth Lay, "A Heidrick & Struggles Interview with Kenneth L. Lay, *The Heidrick & Struggles Leadership Opus: Access and Influence in the 21st Century* (2001): 27.
3. Patrick Butler et al., "A Revolution in Interaction," *McKinsey Quarterly* , no. 1 (1997): 8.
4. Edward E. Lawler III, *Rewarding Excellence: Pay Strategies for the New Economy* (San Francisco: Jossey-Bass, 2000), 112; and McKinsey & Company's War for Technical Talent, a case study of top-quartile software developers versus the other three quartiles.
5. John A. Byrne, "Visionary vs. Visionary," *Business Week,* 28 August 2000, 212.
6. War for Talent (WFT) 2000 Corporate Officer Survey, percentage of respondents who strongly or somewhat agreed with the statements "Three years from now our talent pool needs to be much stronger," and "Our company has enough talented managers to pursue all or most of its promising opportunities."
7. "Former Oracle Leader Now Working with Venture Capital Firm," *USA Today,* 24 August 2000.
8. U.S. Bureau of Labor Statistics, "Labor Force 2008," *Monthly Labor Review* (November 1999); U.S. Census Bureau, *Statistical Abstract of the United States, 1999,* Table 14; and *National Population Projections—Summary Tables* (Washington, DC: GPO, January 2000).
9. Ibid.
10. Murray Gendell, "Trends in Retirement Age in Four Countries, 1965–1995," *Monthly Labor Review* (August 1998).
11. Scott Woody, Johnson & Johnson Sourcing Manager, "Leveraging Technologies to Increase Sourcing and Staffing Effectiveness" (presentation given at the IQPC 3rd Annual Recruiting and Staffing Summit, Scottsdale, AZ, November 2000).

12. Jim Robbins, interview with author, January 2000.

13. Managing Directors of two large international executive search firms, conversations with author, April 2001.

14. WFT 2000 Senior Executive and Midlevel Surveys. Of respondents, 20 percent said there is a 60 percent or greater chance they will leave their company in the next two years; another 28 percent said there is a 30 percent or greater chance.

15. WFT 2000 Survey: Of middle managers under the age of thirty-five, 23 percent said there is a 60 percent or greater chance that they will leave their company in the next two years, versus 14 percent of older senior managers.

16. Peter Cappelli, *The New Deal at Work: Managing the Market-Driven Workforce* (Boston: Harvard Business School Press, 1999), 17, 226.

17. Explanation of the total return to shareholders analysis: Companies' total returns to shareholders were compared to their industry peers, as defined by two-digit Standard Industry Code (SIC). Companies better at talent management were those that had top-quintile scores on McKinsey's talent management composite index. Companies worse at talent management were those that had bottom-quintile scores. The talent management composite index consisted of WFT Survey questions on eight talent topics: talent mindset, performance ethic, employee value proposition, recruiting, retention, open and trusting environment, development, and moving on C players. This analysis was also done with the 1997 survey data and resulted in similar findings.

18. WFT 2000 Corporate Officer, Senior Executive, and Midlevel Surveys, percentage of respondents who strongly agreed with the statements "Winning the war for talent is critical to our company's success," and "We are confident that our current actions will lead to a stronger talent pool in the next three years."

19. Jim Robbins, interview with author, January 2000.

20. WFT Corporate Officer, Senior Executive, and Midlevel Surveys, percentage of respondents that strongly agreed that "Improving the strength of our company's talent pool is currently one of our senior management's top three priorities."

21. Larry Bossidy, "The Job No CEO Should Delegate," *Harvard Business Review* 99, no. 3 (2001): 47–49.

22. WFT 2000 Corporate Officer Survey.

23. WFT 1997 and 2000 Senior Executive Surveys combined, percentage of respondents who strongly agreed with the statement "Our company knows who the high performers and low performers are in the company."

Chapter 2

1. Susan Camaniti, "The New Champs of Retailing," *Fortune*, 24 September 1990, 85–100.

2. Rebecca Quick, "A Make-over That Began at the Top," *Wall Street Journal*, 25 May 2000; and Les Wexner, interview with author, October 2000.

3. WFT 2000 Corporate Officer and Senior Executive Surveys.

4. Nick Gilbert, "CEO of the Year: Larry Bossidy of AlliedSignal," *Financial World*, 29 March 1994, 44–52.

5. PepsiCo, interviews with authors, 1995.

6. WFT 2000 Corporate Officer and Senior Executive Surveys.

7. WFT 2000 Corporate Officer Survey.

8. WFT 2000 Corporate Officer, Senior Executive, and Midlevel Surveys.

9. Ibid.

10. WFT 2000 Corporate Officer Survey.

11. WFT 2000 Corporate Officer and Senior Executive Surveys.

12. McKinsey's Value of Better Talent research, 2000. We studied a manufacturing company, an industrial services firm, and a financial services institution in order to assess the differential impact of better talent (in selected line management positions) across industries. We asked senior managers in each case company to designate which selected line managers were As, Bs, and Cs. We then examined plant or portfolio performance over a multiyear time period, controlling for other variables that might affect their respective performances such as annual macroeconomic and industry-specific fluctuations, company-specific factors, and plant-specific factors. The findings of our research in three companies showed that A players generated between 50 percent and 130 percent revenue or profit growth, while B and C players generated roughly flat performance.

Chapter 3

1. Richard Powers, *Gain: A Novel* (New York: Picador, 1998).

2. We formed eighteen composites, each of which comprised three or four individual survey questions, including the questions shown in figure 3-1. Then we analyzed the composites for their causal relationship with job satisfaction as reported by the individual. The items shown bolded and with check marks in figure 3-1 were the questions from composites that had a strong causal relationship with satisfaction.

3. WFT 2000 Senior Executive and Midlevel Surveys. In figure 3-3, respondents' ratings of their company's delivery on the questions comprising the open and trusting composite and the performance orientation composite were analyzed for a relationship with satisfaction with the company's culture.

4. Hagberg Consulting Group (<www.hagnet.com>) provided us assistance with the culture portion of the WFT 2000 Survey.

5. WFT 2000 Midlevel Survey.

6. Michael Lewis, "Boom or Bust," *Business 2.0*, April 2000.

7. Jennifer Merritt of *Business Week*, interview with author, December 2000. Average starting total compensation for M.B.A.'s from the twenty-five top business schools was $93,630 in 1996 and $126,930 in 2000.

8. Anthony Bianco and Louis Lavelle, "The CEO Trap," *Business Week*, 11

December 2000, 88. Average CEO compensation in large companies was $1.2 million in 1989 and $12.4 million in 1999.

9. See exhibit 6-1 in chapter 6, WFT 2000 Senior Executive and Midlevel Surveys.

10. Edward E. Lawler III, *Rewarding Excellence: Pay Strategies for the New Economy* (San Francisco: Jossey-Bass, 2000), 89–91.

11. Ibid., preface.

12. For further discussion of Generation X, see for example, Robert Barnard, Dave Cosgrave, and Jennifer Welsh, *Chips & Pop: Decoding the Nexus Generation* (Toronto: Malcolm Lester Books, 1998); Bruce Tulgan, *Managing Generation X: How to Bring Out the Best in Young Talent* (New York: Norton, 2000); and Ron Zemke, Claire Raines, and Bob Filipczak, *Generations at Work: Managing the Clash of Veterans, Boomers, Xers, and Nexters in Your Workplace* (New York: AMA-COM, 2000).

13. Robert B. Reich, *The Future of Success* (New York: Knopf, 2001).

14. Michelle Neely Martinez, "Winning Ways to Recruit," *HR Magazine*, June 2000, 56–64.

Chapter 4

1. Robert Lacey, *Ford: The Men and the Machine* (Boston: Little, Brown, 1986), 118.

2. Patti Bond, "Retooling at Home Depot: CEO to Build on 'Winning Formula'—Company's Founders Hand Off to Nardelli," *Atlanta Journal-Constitution*, 6 December 2000.

3. *Business Week* reported that one-third of CEOs appointed at 450 major corporations in the 1990s lasted three years or less ("The CEO Trap," December 11, 2000). Hunt-Scanlon estimates that roughly 35 percent of senior executives hired externally fail to meet the board's expectations within the first two years. (Brian Lee, Chief Marketing Strategist, Hunt-Scanlon, telephone conversation with author, 25 January 2001).

4. In a study of entry-level auditors in large public accounting firms, Jennifer Chatman, a professor at Berkeley's Haas School of Business, found important benefits of using cultural fit as a selection criterion. Her research revealed that how closely recruits' values at the time of hire matched those of their firm predicted how satisfied they were with their firm one year later and how likely they were to quit within the first two-and-a-half years. For more information, see her study: Jennifer A. Chatman, "Matching People and Organizations: Selection and Socialization in Public Accounting Firms," *Administrative Science Quarterly* 36 (1991): 459–484.

5. Newman Korn, "Gotcha!," *Across the Board*, September 1998.

6. Gina Imperato, "How to Hire the Next Michael Jordan," *Fast Company*, December 1998, 212.

7. Christine Willard, "For Sale: One IT staff," *Computerworld*, 30 August 1999, 52;

Scott Hays, "Sears Turns Office Space into a Recruiting Tool," *Workforce*, December 1998, 117–120.

8. Dee Hock, quoted by Greg Barnes, "Talent Crunch Gets Personal in Today's Tight Job Market," *Houston Business Journal*, 4 September 2000.

9. WFT 2000 Senior Executive and Midlevel Surveys. Of mid- and senior-level managers, 48 percent said there is a 30 percent or greater chance of leaving their current employer in the next two years.

10. WFT 2000 Senior Executive and Midlevel Surveys. Sixty-four percent of the managers who left their previous company in the last three years did so because a better offer came their way.

11. Jerry Useem, "For Sale Online: You," *Fortune*, 5 July 1999, 66–78.

12. Ibid., 70.

13. Anna Muoio, "Man with a (Talent) Plan," *Fast Company*, January 2001, 83–89.

14. Adam Bryant, "MBA: Managed By Agent," *Newsweek*, 17 May 1999, 54.

15. WFT 1997 Senior Executive Survey.

16. Rachel Emma Silverman, "The Jungle," *The Wall Street Journal*, 11 July 2000; and "Japanese Network Security Firm Seeking Hackers," Jiji Press Ticker Service, 15 February 1999.

Chapter 5

1. J. Sterling Livingston, "Pygmalion in Management," *Harvard Business Review* 66, no. 5 (1988): 121–130.

2. WFT 2000 Corporate Officer Survey.

3. WFT 2000 Corporate Officer, Senior Executive, and Midlevel Surveys, percentage of respondents who strongly or somewhat disagreed that their company develops people quickly and effectively.

4. WFT 2000 Senior Executive and Midlevel Surveys. Forty-seven percent of the managers who strongly disagreed that their company develops people quickly and effectively said there is a 60 percent or greater chance of their leaving their company; in contrast, only 10 percent of the managers who strongly agreed that their company develops people quickly and effectively said there is a 60 percent or greater chance of their leaving.

5. WFT 2000 Senior Executive and Midlevel Surveys.

6. WFT 2000 Senior Executive and Midlevel Surveys, percentage of respondents who said their company was either "excellent" or "good" at delivering these components of development.

7. See, for example, John P. Kotter, *The Leadership Factor* (New York: Free Press, 1988); Morgan W. McCall, Jr., Michael M. Lombardo, and Ann M. Morrison, *The Lessons of Experience: How Successful Executives Develop on the Job* (Lexington, MA: Lexington Books, 1988).

8. Livingston, "Pygmalion in Management," 129.

9. McCall, Lombardo, and Morrison, *The Lessons of Experience*, 15–65.

10. Johnson & Johnson 2000 Facts, <www.JJ.com>.

11. WFT 1997 Senior Manager Survey.

12. GE, like most companies, has an internal job-posting system for the people below the top 500. We are talking here about the deployment decisions for the top 500 people.

13. Morgan W. McCall, Jr., *High Flyers: Developing the Next Generation of Leaders* (Boston: Harvard Business School Press, 1998), chapter 2, 21–59.

14. WFT 2000 Corporate Officer, Senior Executive, and Midlevel Surveys, percentage of respondents who strongly or somewhat agreed with the statement, "People are told candidly and frankly where they stand at our company."

15. McCall, *High Flyers,* 177.

16. WFT 2000 Senior Executive and Midlevel Surveys, percentage of respondents who strongly or somewhat agreed with the cited statements.

17. Mentoring research conducted in 2000 by McKinsey & Company and John Roth of the McCallie School, Chattanooga, Tennessee.

18. WFT Corporate Officer, Senior Executive, and Midlevel Surveys, percentage of respondents who strongly or somewhat agreed with these statements about mentoring.

19. Shari Caudron, "Learning Revives Training," *Workforce,* January 2000, 34–37.

20. Jonathan Rosen, *The Talmud and the Internet* (New York: Farrar, Straus & Giroux, 2000), 34.

Chapter 6

1. John Terraine, *A Time for Courage: The Royal Air Force in the European War, 1939–1945* (New York: Macmillan, 1985).

2. WFT 2000 Senior Executive and Midlevel Surveys. For the statement "In my company, I am recognized and rewarded appropriately for my individual contribution," the percentage of respondents who indicated this factor as being "critical" or "very important" to their decision to join or stay with their company.

3. WFT 2000 Senior Executive and Midlevel Surveys. Statistical correlation between affirmation questions ("My company demonstrates a long-term commitment to me," "In my company, I am recognized and rewarded appropriately for my individual contribution," and "My company is quick to recognize and reward me for the contributions I make") and greater satisfaction/less likelihood of leaving the company was demonstrated.

4. WFT 2000 Corporate Officer, Senior Executive, and Midlevel Surveys.

5. Ibid.

6. WFT 2000 Corporate Officer Survey.

7. Procter & Gamble information from Dave Zielinski, "Mentoring Up," *Training,*

October 2000, 136–140. Hewlett-Packard information from original McKinsey case research, 1997.

8. Brush Dance catalogue (Mill Valley, CA, 1999), 18.

9. WFT 2000 Senior Executive and Midlevel Surveys. Of the 58 percent of respondents who have worked for a C player, the percentage who strongly or somewhat agreed with the following statements: "Hurt my career development," 81 percent; "Prevented me from learning," 76 percent; "Prevented me from making a larger contribution to the company's bottom line," 82 percent; and "Made me want to leave the company," 85 percent.

10. George Anders, "Marc Andreessen: Act II," *Fast Company*, February 2001, 110.

11. WFT 2000 Senior Executive and Midlevel Survey. In companies that do not manage underperformers effectively, only 35 percent of respondents think their company is well managed, as opposed to 78 percent in companies that do move effectively on underperformers.

12. McKinsey's Value of Better Talent research, 2000.

13. WFT 2000 Corporate Officers Survey, percentage of respondents citing the following as "huge" or "major" obstacles to taking action on C players: "Senior managers are unwilling to fire or move aside people who have contributed and 'met expectations' for many years," 72 percent; "Senior managers are unwilling to move aside or fire the people they have worked with for many years," 70 percent.

14. Ram Charan and Geoffrey Colvin, "Why CEOs Fail," *Fortune*, 21 June 1999, 68–78.

15. A phrase attributed to Napoleon, who said, "Men must be led by an iron hand in a velvet glove." It is an image of absolute firmness made more palatable and effective through courtesy and manners.

16. WFT 2000 Corporate Officer Survey.

17. Based on interviews with CEO Frank Cicutto and other executives of the National Australia Bank during the period December 2000 to April 2001.

Chapter 7

1. WFT 2000 Corporate Officer, Senior Executive, and Midlevel Surveys.

2. WFT 2000 Corporate Officer Survey.

3. Ibid.

4. Mike Ruettgers, interview with author, 2000.

INDEX

ABOUT THE AUTHORS

Ed Michaels, a Director in McKinsey & Company's Atlanta office, has concentrated the last ten years of his consulting career on improving clients' growth strategies and strengthening their talent pools. In 1994, he established McKinsey's War for Talent practice and co-led the original 1997 War for Talent research. He has served more than thirty clients on talent-related issues and has addressed dozens of forums on the strategic advantage of excellent talent management. In August 1998, Charles Fishman's interview with Michaels in *Fast Company* helped popularize the War for Talent concepts. Michaels retired in June 2001, after thirty-two years with McKinsey.

Helen Handfield-Jones is a Senior Practice Expert with McKinsey & Company's Organization practice, with a focus in talent management. She co-led the original 1997 War for Talent research and has been one of the leaders of McKinsey's War for Talent practice since 1994. Based in Toronto, Handfield-Jones has led workshops with senior leaders in more than thirty companies and has advised many client teams around the world on talent and performance management. She speaks to many forums on the War for Talent, including Wharton's Leadership Conference and Cornell University's International Human Resource Executive Development Program.

Beth Axelrod, a Principal in McKinsey & Company's Stamford, Connecticut office, has served clients across a variety of industries for twelve years on business strategy and organization issues. Over the past three years, she has counseled more than thirty companies on talent strategy. Axelrod is currently the leader of the War for Talent practice and is one of the leaders of McKinsey's global Organization and Leadership practice. She led the 2000 War for Talent research. Axelrod speaks frequently to companies and conferences about talent issues, including the Conference Board and the Human Resource Planning Society.

Collectively the three authors have published widely on talent management topics. Articles on their research and thinking have been published in *Fast Company*, the *Harvard Business Review*, *Leader to Leader*, the *McKinsey Quarterly*, and the *Globe and Mail.* The War for Talent research findings have been presented at the Davos World Economic Forum. Along with their War for Talent team, the authors received the 2000 PRO award honoring individuals who made a major contribution to the development of the HR management field from the International Association of Professional and Corporate Recruiters.